Them and Us

Memories of Upper and Lower Wolvercote 1900 - 1980

Michael H. Stockford

Published on behalf of the author by
Robert Boyd Publications
260 Colwell Drive
Witney, Oxfordshire OX28 5LW

First published 2011

ISBN: 978 1 908738 01 1

*Copies of theis book are available from the author at
3 Bishop Kirk Place, Woodstock Road
Oxford OX2 7HJ*

Printed and bound by
Information Press, Southfield Road, Eynsham
Oxford OX29 4JB

Contents

Front cover illustrations - a journey through Wolvercote

Trout bridge • Toll bridge bathing • Baptist Church
Red Lion • Paper Mill • White Hart • Railway crossing • The Canal
The Plough • St Peter's Church • School House

Back cover illustration

The Bellamy Memorial Window, designed by John Piper
and made by Patrick Reyntiens, 1976.

They took branches of palm trees and went out to meet him.
John 12, 13

UPPER WOLVERCOTE RESIDENTS 1934.

FIRST TURN (Wolvercote), from 385 Woodstock road to Green road.

NORTH SIDE.
Davis Philip ('The Mere')
Rebbeck Rev. Paul Edwd. M.A. [vicar of St. Peter's, Wolvercote] (The Vicarage)
CHURCH OF ST. PETER
...... here is *Church la* ...
Cox Miss (The Studio)
Gallaway Chas. (The Old School)
King Hy, Osborn, hay mer. (Church farm)
...... here is *Green rd* ......

SOUTH SIDE.
Annetts Lancelot Geo. (Elmcot)
BLENHEIM VILLAS:
1 Taylor Miss
2 WinstoneWm.Ethelbert
Fallows Wm. Thos. Hy. (School ho)
Council School (mixed & infants)
Dunaresq Miss(The Upper farm)
White Ernest (Ivy cott)
CYPRESS TERRACE :
9 Stone Arth
8 Collett Fredk
7 Beesley Bertie Orlando
6 Weston Geo
5 Day Mrs
4 Crooks Mrs
3 Allen Mrs
2 Mott Wm
1 Saxton Edwl. Geo

GREEN ROAD (Wolvercote), from Church road.

EAST SIDE.
Plough inn, Jn. Wiltr. Stockford
1 Venney Alfd. Gordon
2 Mott Mrs
3 Hathaway Wm. Thos
4 Gurney Chas. Wm. Hy
5 Simmons Mrs
6 Thompson Leslie H
7 Pether Gilbt. Edwd
9 Mitchell Wm
10 Cooper Mrs
11 Fry Mrs
12 Ody Percvl. Gordon
WESTVIEW COTTAGES :
1 Hillsdon Mrs
2 Cummings Wiltr
3 Hewlett Mrs
4 Loveridge Ernest
5 Loveridge Ernest
Woodward Jsph. Hy
Haskins Jsph
Hastings Chas
Howard Geo
SHUFFREY'S YARD:
Savins Mrs
Collins Wm
Jones Rd
Warwick Chas
Ody Gordon
Moss Fredk
Wain Hy
Gregory Geo

SOUTH SIDE.
Bennett Graham
...... *here is entrance to Council houses*......
Walker Jn. (Lower Farm cott)
Underwood Geo. Alex. (Lower Farm cott)

NORTH SIDE.
Honour Mrs. M. H. farmer (Manor farm)
...... here is *The Green*......

GREEN (THE) (Wolvercote), from Godstow road.
Axtell Wm
Cross Mrs
Brooks Chas
Adams Bertram
3 Newnes Wm. Hy
Payne Stanley
Lewis Benj

CHURCHILL PLACE, Upper Wolvercote. From Mere road.
1 Bourne Mrs
2 Wyatt Christphr
3 Stockford
4 Loveridge Edwd
5 Smith Arth
6 Stanley Fredk. W. grocr

NORTH SIDE.
North Oxford Brick Co. brick mfrs
Clements Thos. Hy. (Brick Works cott)
Freeman Mrs
Hutt Mrs. Alfd
Green Thos
Hutt Mrs. C

FIVE MILE DRIVE (Wolvercote), from Woodstock road to Banbury rd.

NORTH SIDE.
Hobson Mrs (Green view)
Hobson Miss D,riding sch
Short Bertram(2Green vw)
Adams Jesse
Mott Thos.,(Rose cott)
Clinkard Wm. H.;market gardener
...... *here are Williams la.* ?

SOUTH SIDE.
Radford David (Northfield)
Woods Wltr. (Greenway)
Smith Wltr. Jn. (The Nook)
Angel Reginld. Jn. (Padua)
Fowler Frank Jn. (Midways)

CHURCH LANE (Wolvercote), from First Turn to 12 Green road.
Pettefer Thos. (Church ho)
Saxton Harold (The Close)

LOWER WOLVERCOTE RESIDENTS 1934.

GODSTOW RD. (Wolvercote), from High street to the Trout inn.

NORTH SIDE.
Honour Mrs. M. H. farmer (Manor farm)
...... here is *The Green*......
Parker Edwd. Chas
Warmington Abel
Parsons Percy
Curtis Austin
Aldsworth Arth
Phipps Fred
Freeman Fredk. shopkpr. & parish clerk
...... here is *Elmthorpe rd* ...
Simms Wltr Hy. grocer
Stockford Chas. (Avalon)
Collett Mrs
Collett Sidney (Lyndhurst)
Collett Aug. D.(Belvedere)
Viner Edwin Gerard
Hope Geo. W
Allen Ernest,farmer (Bedford House farm)
Kingzett Miss Harriett
Le Clerc Rt. Maurice L.M., L.S.,D.,b. physcn. & surg. (surgery)
Cross Jn. Wm.,hairdrssr
Goldsworthy Frank Alex
Fleetwood Arth
Medcraft Fredk. Jn
Saxton Edwin Geo. blacksmith
Thompson Arth
Chamberlain Harry
White Hart P.H. Saml. Green
Cooling Wm. F. J. carrier

Chamberlain Jas. Wm. shopkpr. & post office
...... here is *Mill rd* ......
Red Lion P. H. Mrs. Rosaline Weston
Medcalfe Wltr
Hastings Wm
Mitchell Mrs
Hewlett Christphr. Jn
Stone Frank
Phipps Ernest
Buckingham Wm
Brown Thos
Cross Chas. Wm
Stone Jn
Hewlett Wm. Edwd
Hutt Alfd
Mapson Jn
Long Wm. (Woodland)
Wharton Fredk
Warmington Wm.(Sunrise)
Clements Mrs
Hambridge Frank Percy

SOUTH SIDE.
Bennett Graham
...... *here is entrance to Council houses*......
Walker Jn. (Lower Farm cott)
...... here is *Green rd* ......
Wren Miss (Thatched cott)
MEADOW VIEW COTTS.:
1 Dean Jn
2 Carter Miss
3 Slatter Fredk
4 Wren Mark
5 Hutt Mrs
6 Stanley Mrs
7 Belcher Jsph
8 Long Alfd
Cole Jas. (The Cot)
Allen W. W. & Sons, haulage contrctrs.(Highbury)
THE ROOKERY :
Wharton Jn
Cooling Alfd. Geo
Savage Hy. Chas
1 Pettifer Mrs
2 Cox Fras. Wm
3 Bidmead Geo

THE ROOKERY, GODSTOW ROAD—continued.
4 Waine Mrs
5 Clementa Saml
6 Collett Leslie
7 Long Wltr
8 Garner Herbt
———
Allen Miss
Thompson Mrs. Ellen
Launchbury Geo. Wm
Howard Wm. Jn
Long Wm. (Wyoming)
Bird Colin (Windyridge)
Saxton Wm. (Ivy Dene)
Higgins Hy.(Laurel Dene)
Taylor Percy B
Waine Hy., (Rosslyn)
Freeman Mrs
Oxford Hunting & Polo Stables
Thomas David(The Lawn)
French Frank Edwd. (Meadow View ho)
Cheeshire Wm. Geo
Stanley Miss
Oliver Albt
Tollett Mrs
Smith Dawson
Matthews Mrs
BAPTIST CHAPEL
Collett Danl
Robinson Wm
Collett Horace
Warmington Saml
Bayliss Miss
Collett Mrs
Lines Miss
French Jas. (The Orchard)
Musto Hy., Jn. jun
Wickson Mrs
Eadle Geo. Hy
Hewlett Wm
Weston Geo
Robinson Hy.,Chas,coal dlr
Robinson Geo. W. (Myrtle villa)
Stone Wm. J. (Hill view)
Willis Alfd. Hy. (Lacolle)
Matthews Christphr
Collett Ralph
Watson Jsph
Matthews Chas. Hv
Robinson Fredk. W. dairyman (The Nook)
BINFIELD HOUSE :
1 Slade Jim
2 Johnson Jsph
3 Higgs Thos

ELMTHORPE ROAD (Wolvercote), from Godstow road. [No thoroughfare.]

EAST SIDE.
1 Allen Mrs. H
2 Cross Jn. Wm
oxf.
3 Medcroft Wm
4 Panting Wm. Jas
5 Collett Fredk. Chas
6 Williams Harry
7 Lee Edwd
8 Morgan Mrs
9 Parsons Ernest
10 Hollifield Sidney
11 Drewett Hy. Jas
12 Taylor Stephen
13 Hollant Geo. Fredk
14 Hall Vernon
15 Collett Percy Thos
Millard Horace(Victoria cott)
16A, Henwood Eden
18 Eastbury Miss Amy
19 Coates Arth Hy
20 Nevin Thos
21 Trafford Harry
Waine Ernest (Northcote)
WEST SIDE.
22 Stanford Edwt
Lovegrove Wm. (Droitwich villa)
23 Collett Jesse
24 Butler Fredk
25 Howard Mrs
26 Tipton Geo
27 Hall Percy
28 Wild Harold
29 Westbury Geo
Trafford Ernest (The Bungalow)
Leach Wm. Hy. (East view)
31 Moulder Jas. Fredk
32 Howard Mrs
33 Eatwell Edwin
Hastings Hy. (Gable)
36 Rance Arth. Wm
37 Trafford Albt. haulage contrctr
Innes Edwd. (Moordown)
40 Allen Mrs
41 Tuffley Mrs
42 Belcher Edwl. Thos

MILL ROAD (Wolvercote), from Godstow road.

NORTH SIDE.
Loveridge Wm
Lines Thos. Wm
Howard Reuben
Wren Harry Alfd
Clapperton Douglas Alex. (Mill ho)
Wolvercote Paper Mills (Douglas A. Clapperton)
SOUTH SIDE.
1 Trafford Jesse
2 Lines Hy
3 Long Chas
4 Lines Wn
5 Chamberlain Mrs
6 Duck Ernest
7 Smith Louis
Fathers Joshua
Carter Percy
Long Herbt
Woodward Herbt

[Trout P.H. Ernest Geo. Coleman]

UPPER WOLVERCOTE RESIDENTS 1943.

FIRST TURN,
Wolvercote.
From 385 Woodstock road to Wolvercote green.
North side.
Ince Mrs. (Fairlawn)
...... here is Mere rd ......
Rebbeck Rev. Paul Edwd. M.A. (vicar of St. Peter's, Wolvercote) (The Vicarage)
Church of St. Peter
... here is Church la ......
Pettefer Thos. (Church ho)
Saxton Harold (The Close)
...
King Hy. Osborn (exors. of), hay mers
King Mrs. (Church farm)
...... here is Green rd ......
South side.
1 Rice Edwd. Marshall
3 Jones Lewis Jas
5 Winstone Wm. Ethelbert
Fallows Wm. Thos. Hy. (School ho)
Council School (mixed & infants)
... here is St. Peter's rd ...
19 White Ernest
21 Finch Wm
23 Smith Stephen W
25 Dodd Jsph. Fras
27 Sutton Noel
29 Spry Arth. Jn
31 Turner Mrs
...
33 Hopkins Herbt. Jas
35 Gregory Geo. W
37 Plough P.H. Jn. Wltr. Stockford
..here is Wolvercote green..

WOLVERCOTE GREEN
Wolvercote.
From Godstow road.
East side.
Wolvercote Village Hall (G. H. Diddams, hon. sec)
5 Revell Stanley Webster
7 Drinkwater Cyril
9 Adams Jesse
13 Hobson Mrs
17 Stevens Miss E. K
19 Grant Sidney Jas
21 Rosser Stanley
... here are Osborne close & Church la ...

OSBORNE CLOSE.
From 21 Wolvercote green Wolvercote.
1 Stibbe Jn
3 Pettett Miss
3 Smith Miss V
4 Waight Mrs
5 Wheatley Cecil J

WOLVERCOTE GREEN
27 Clemson Frank
29 Sanders Geo. Hy
31 Humphris Hubert H
33 Smith Arth
35 Ward Edwin
37 Loveridge Edwd
39 Mott Mrs
41 Venney Alfd. Gordon
...... here is First turn ....
55 Hastings Chas
57 Haskins Mrs
59 Stroudley Wm

CHURCHILL PLACE,
(Upper Wolvercote), from Williams lane.
1 Bourne Mrs
2 Pettifer Mrs
3 Hathaway Wm. Thos
4 Gurney Chas. Wm. Hy
5 Simmons Mrs
6 Thompson Leslie H
7 Pether Gilbt. Edwd
8 Howard Wm. Jn
9 Mitchell Wm
10 Cooper Mrs
11 Fry Mrs
12 Ody Percvl. Gordon

MERE ROAD,
Wolvercote.
From First turn to Godstow road.
East side.
2 Earnshaw Lawrence
4 Brockington Guy
6 Franklin Rt
8 Ruscoe Wilfred
10 Davies Norman Douglas
12 Hillyard Hugh
14 Spoor Mrs
16 Whomsley Geo. Leslie
West side.
... here is Churchill pl .....

GODSTOW ROAD,
Wolvercote.
From Woodstock road.
North side.
26 Goode Edwd. Leonard
... here is Wolvercote grn ...
here is bridge over railway
South side.
1 Bennett Graham B.Sc
7 Frost Frank Jn
9 Hawkins Albt. Jas
11 Hudson Cecil H
13 Miles Jack A
15 Lee Edmnd
17 Sellers Kenneth
......here are Mere & Green roads......
here is bridge over railway

PIXEY PLACE,
Wolvercote.
From Ulfgar road.
(No thoroughfare.)
1 Pettefer Jsph
3 Buckle Ernest Jas
5 Turner Mrs
7 Hallett Mrs
9 Plato Raymond Geo
11 Duffin Chas. L
13 Soden Leonard
15 Dorrill Lewis E
17 Warwick Ernest, jun
19 Murphy Thos
21 Taylor Arth. Geo
23 Warwick Chas. sen

ST. PETER'S ROAD,
Wolvercote.
From First Turn to 33 Ulfgar road.
East side.
1 Buckingham Wm
3 Hill Wm. Jsph
5 Fawdrey Edgar
7 Morgan Albt. Denis
9 Stone Fras. Rd. Jas
11 Henton Wm
13 Powney Hy. Chas
15 Castle Edwd. Geo
17 Lewis Ben Edgar E
19 Bell Jas
21 Knight Sam
23 Smithson Geo
25 Mazey Mrs
27 Fletcher Thos. Edwd
29 Prescott Norman Chas
31 Quarterman Fras. F
33 Ferguson Thos
35 Drinkwater Mrs
37 Hughes Jn
39 Jones Mrs
41 Burgess Wm. Jn
43 Payne Stanley Rt
45 Smith Thos. Rd
47 Owen Philip
49 Noonan Michl
51 Wells Wltr
West side.
First Turn Stores (Cecil R. Eyres, propr.), grocer, & post office

Cyprus Terrace.
1 Saxton Edwd. Geo
2 Mott Wm
3 Herring Wm. Edwd
4 Crook Miss
5 Day Cyril
6 Stone Alex
7 Beesley Bertie Orlando
8 Collett Fredk
9 Stone Arth
—
Community Centre (Mrs. E. N. C. Sergeant, sec.) (The Upper farm)
Bevan Geo. Ernest (The Upper farm)
...... here is Ulfgar rd ......
2 Allen Alfd
4 Walker Wltr
6 Hoare Horace
8 Walton Percvl
10 Hopkins Jas
12 Clare Cyril Jn
14 Hitks Thos
16 Axtell Mrs
18 Cheshire Wm. Geo
20 Collett Mrs
22 Chadwick Jas. Wltr

ULFGAR ROAD.
Wolvercote.
From 2 St. Peter's road.
East side.
1 Knight Wm
3 Thompson Miss J
5 Howse Jn
7 Dunsby Bert
9 Pratley Mrs
11 Keen Albt. Edwd
13 Pettifer Mrs. E
15 Cox Fras. Wm
17 Waine Jn
19 Howell Mrs. G
21 Dawson Fredk
23 Walker Jn
25 O'Neill Hy. Jsph
27 Blackwell Mrs
29 Hughes Jas. G
31 Collett Frank
...... here is St. Peter's rd ....
33 Jones Wm. Hy
35 Chandler Mrs
37 Jones Stanley Reames
39 Simms Gilbt. Stanley
41 Brockall Harry Rt. C
43 Richardson Jn
45 Portman Regnld. G
47 Duncan Albt. Ernest
West side.
.... here is Pixey pl ....
10 Dawson Mrs. S
12 Miller Sidney
14 Witchard Wm. Jn
16 Halsey Percy
18 Loveridge Mrs. E. K
20 Styles Fredk
22 Wigley Rd
24 Waine Mrs. E
26 Hastings Mrs. L
28 Viner Mrs. A
30 Townsend Mrs
32 Woodward Jsph
34 Bidmead Herbt. Geo
36 Robbins Leslie Arth
38 Savage Simeon C. W
40 Fitzgerald Fredk
42 Cummings Geo
44 Long Wltr
46 Drinkwater Edwd
48 Lambert Arth
50 Matthews Harry
52 Savage Peter Fredk
54 Aldsworth Ernest Fredk
56 Gold Herbt
58 Cox Jn
60 Mott Cecil
62 Loveridge Ernest
64 Tyler Lionel
66 Standingford Wm. Chas
68 Howard Geo. Ernest
70 Williamson Arth. Jas
72 Weston Geo. Jas
74 Collett Horace J
76 Fidler Mrs
78 Wharton Mrs
80 Clarke Ronald A
82 Gardner Gilbt. Jas
84 Haynes Jas. Edwd
86 Carter Mrs

FIVE MILE DRIVE
(Wolvercote), from Woodstock road to Banbury rd.
NORTH SIDE.
84 Clements Thos. Hy
82 Mitchell Frank
80 Potter Mrs. Florence
78 Brown Miss M. R
76 Launchbury Regnld
74 Hardacre Geoffrey R
72 Griffin Ernest Edwd
72 Griffin Ellis & Sons, plasterers. Telephone No. Oxford 58568
.....here is Carey close......
70 Alexander Chas
68 Frost Cyril Stanley
66 Meeking Miss K
64 Higgs Wm. Reeve
62 Smee Thos. Geo
60 Bradley Denis Geo
58 Grose Hy. Chas
56 Axtell Ed. Jn
54 Knibbs Wltr. Geo
52 Freeman Mrs
50 Hutt Wltr. Thos. Herbt
48 Green Thos
46 Hutt Mrs. C
44 Clements Fredk
42 Rowland Miss
..... here is Linkside av ....
40 Watson Graham
38 Bridges Wilfred T. R
36 Plested Aubrey Sinclair
34 Sanders Wilfrid Thos
32 Blanton Philip
30 Baker Mrs
28 Powell Cecil M
26 Gilbert Donald V
Oxford High School Playing Fields

SOUTH SIDE.
83 Milnes Rev. Jn. Harrison M.A. (bursar Mansfield College)
81 Cranage Mrs
79 Nash Chas. Hy. Jn
77 Griffiths Sydney
73 Langford Harry
71 Woods Hubert
67 Ives Miss O. M
65 Smith Wm. Jn
63 Vasey Chas. Hy
61 Watson Miss Mary S
59 Chappell Rev. Geo. T. M.A
57 Franks Mrs. Ada
55 Hay Ian M
53 Holmden Edwd. H
51 Fowler Frank Jn
49 Dawes Benj
47 Ward Mrs
41 Neat Paym. Capt. Edwd. Hugh C.M.G., R.N. (ret)
39 Blatherwick Hy
37 Phillips Leonard C. W
35 Dyke Frank E
33 Butterfield Alec Robin
31 Walker Frank Wm
29 Nethercott Arth. Wm
25 Burrows Wltr. Frank
23 Rogerson Oswald
21 Guinness Rev. Arth. Rt. Hy. M.A
19 Jones Kenneth
17 Phillips Mrs. E
15 Robinson Jn. Geo
13 Alben Ernest
11 Guy Regnld. W
Minty Mrs. G. M. (Wroxeter)
Smith Thos. F. (Norvic)
5 Rose Thos. Alfd

NOTE:- I appreciate that Five Mile Drive is not Wolvercote (although in the parish) but have included it purely to indicate the corresponding growth in population.

LOWER WOLVERCOTE RESIDENTS 1943.

GODSTOW ROAD,
Wolvercote.

From Woodstock road.

North side.

26 Goode Edwd. Leonard
... here is Wolvercote grn ...
here is bridge over railway
46 Parker Mrs
48 Warmington Abel
50 Parsons Percy
52 Curtis Austin
54 Aldsworth Mrs
56 Waine Wm. Thos
58 West Mrs. Maud D. shop-
     keeper
... here is Elmthorpe rd ...
60 Simms Wltr. H. shopkpr
62 Stockford Chas
64 Collett Mrs
66 Young Thos
68 Collett Aug. D
70 Viner Edwin Gerard
72 Gillett Hy. confctnr
74 Heselton Hy
74 Heselton Mrs. Nora L.
     ladies' hairdrssr
76 Stevens Geo
78 Smith Fredk. Jas
80 Frith Wm. B
82 Bowles Ralph J. grocer,
     & post office
... here is Rosamund rd ...
84 Gibson Geo. & Son,
     butchers
86 Peachey Mrs. Louisa
88 Philpott Albt. Wm
90 Weston Frank Herbt
92 Drewett Arth. J
102 Matthews Chas. Hy
.....here is Home close......
104 Beesley Leonard R.
     shopkpr
106 Surman Victor Chas.
     fried fish shop
108 French Jas
110 Cross Jn. Wm. cycle repr

112 Goldsworthy Frank A
114 Walker Jn
118 Medcraft Fredk. Jn
120 Saxton Mrs
122 Thompson Arth
124 Chamberlain Harry
126 White Hart P.H. Hy
     W. Hastings
128 Couling Wm. Fredk. J
     haulage contrctr
.........here is Mill rd........
130 Red Lion P.H. Gilbt
     Lewis Rivers
144 Medcraft Mrs
146 Hastings Wm
148 Trafford Ernest Albt
158 Brown Thos
160 Cross Chas. Wm
164 Stone Jn
166 Anderson Geo. Victor
188 Hutt Alfd
190 Mapson Jn
...here is bridge over river..
216 Long Wm
218 Howard Jsph. Edwd
222 Bond Mrs. A.L. shopkpr
224 Warmington Mrs
226 Clements Mrs
228 Hambridge Percy

South side.

1 Bennett Graham B.Sc
7 Frost Frank Jn
9 Hawkins Albt. Jas
11 Hudson Cecil H
13 Miles Jack A
15 Lee Edmnd
17 Sellers Kenneth
......here are Mere & Green
     roads......
here is bridge over railway
49 Fowler Wm. Jas
51 Carter Miss
53 Gibson Geo
55 Lloyd David
57 Hutt Mrs
59 Panting Mrs
61 & 63 Long Alfd
65 Freeman Mrs
67 Allen W. W. & Sons,
     coal mers
71 Savage Hy
77 Allen Miss
79 Thompson Mrs. Ellen
81 Launchbury Geo. Wm
83 Howard Wm. Jn
85 Long Wm
87 James Edwd
89 Hall Ernest
91 Higgins Wm. Hy
93 Taylor Chas
95 Taylor Percvl. Chas
97 Waine Hy

MILL ROAD,
Wolvercote.

From Godstow road.

North side.

Chamberlain Mrs. Louisa,
     shopkpr

Mill Cottages.

1 Loveridge Mrs
2 Parsons Cyril
3 Belcher Eric
4 Wren Harry Alfd

Clapperton Douglas Alex.
     (Mill ho)
Wolvercote Paper Mills
     (Douglas A. Clapperton).

South side.

Saxton Edwin G. black-
     smith
1 Trafford Jesse
2 Lines Hy
3 Lines Thos. Wm
4 Lines Wm
5 Henwood Eden
6 Duck Ernest
7 Coles Stanley C
8 Wren Mark
9 Mortimer Cyril Arth
10 Olley Jn. Wm
11 Long Herbt

99 Freeman Mrs
101 Phipps Wltr. Edwd.
     M.R.C.V.S., Capt.
     R.A.V.C. (R.O.), veter-
     inary surgn
101 Webster Geo. Noel
103 Tarry Chas. W
105 Brain Jn
105 Hoey Jn. Trevor Steven-
     son M.A., B.M., B.Ch.,
     M. R. C. S. Eng.,
     L.R.C.P. Lond. physcn.
     & surgn. (surgery)
..here is Meadow Prospect..
107 Tapsell Wltr. Jsph
109 Watmough Mark
111 Cornish Alfd. Edwd
113 Beardsley Jn. W
115 Collett Albt
117 Hutchison Geo
119 Robinson Alfd. G. dairy
     man
121 Oliver Albt
125 Tollett Mrs
127 Matthews Geo
     Baptist Chapel
131 Cripps Oliver Hy
133 Robinson Wm
135 Collett Horace
137 Warmington Saml
139 Bayliss Miss
143 Turner Thos. Fredk
145 Lines Miss
155 Long Chas
157 Neale Gilbt. Geo
159 Loch Rt. Hugh
161 Peachey Mrs
163 Higgs Miss A
165 Hicks Mrs. E
167 Robinson Hy. G. coal
     mer
169 Robinson W
171 Stone Wm. J
173 Willis Alfd. Hy
175 Cox Ernest
177 Collett Ralph
179 Collett Alfd
181 Higgs Thos
183 Serman Gordon
185 Robinson Mrs. F
187 Wilkins Wm. Hy. M.A.,
     D.Phil. (University
     demonstrator & lec-
     turer in botany, tutor
     in natural science, St.
     Peter's hall; lecturer
     in botany, Queen's
     college; & lecturer in
     natural science, Hert-
     ford college)
..here is bridge over river..

193 St. Edward's School
     Boathouse
     Trout Inn, Mrs. H. H.
     Coleman

ELMTHORPE ROAD,
Wolvercote.

From 58 Godstow road.
(No thoroughfare.)

East side.

2 Thompson Stanley
4 Cross Jn. Wm
6 Medcraft Wm. Jn
8 Coy Geo. Fredk
10 Collett Fredk. Chas
12 Williams Hy. Louis
14 Stone Ernest
16 Stokes Fredk. Hy
18 Parsons Albt. Frank
19 Holifield Sidney
22 Drewett Hy. Jas
24 Taylor Mrs
26 Stowe Jn. Wm
28 Belcher Jsph
34 Collett Percy Thos
36 Weaver Wm. Sydney
38 Sussex Mrs. C. R
40 Newport Ronald
42 Mortimer Percy
44 Coates Arth. Hy
46 Nevin Thos
48 Trafford Harry
50 Waine Mrs

West side.

51 Tipton Mrs
49 Lovegrove Wm
47 Allen Ronald Chas
45 Butler Fredk
43 Simmonds Albt
41 Eadle Geo
39 Tuffley Wm. Thos
37 Wild Harold
35 Westbury Geo
27 Westow Wm
25 Walker Jn
23 Moulder Jas. Fredk
21 Hewlett Mrs. R. B
19 Stone Edwd
17 Hall Arth
15 Rance Arth. Wm
13 Trafford Albt
13 Trafford A. & Sons, haul-
     age contrctrs
7 Innes Miss A
5 Allen Mrs
3 Tuffley Mrs
1 Belcher Edwd. Thos

MEADOW PROSPECT,
Wolvercote.

From 105 Godstow road.
(No thoroughfare.)

East side.

1 Gomm Jsph. Arth
3 Collett Desmond
5 Allsop Thos
7 Kirkley Wm
9 Evans Wm. Fredk
11 Fidler Ronald
13 Stringer Alfd. Geo
15 French Frank Edwd
17 Crozier Fras. Colin
19 Turner Wm. Geo. Edwd
21 Parker Kenneth Geo
23 Spiers Fras. Chas
25 Hewlett Christphr. Jn
27 Hill Leonard Hy
29 Gatz Bernard Wm
31 Flynn Jn. Jsph
33 Warmington Arth. L
35 Warmington C. Jas
37 Howard Ronald Roy
39 Battrick Albt
41 Millard Albt. Wm
43 Millard Horace Eugene
45 Alderman Edwin Geo
47 Kilby Edwd
49 Jones Wm. Alfd
51 Brooks Arth. Lionel
53 Prince Mrs
55 Honey Hubert

West side.

6 Pitson Albt. Geo
8 Saunders Rt
10 Kynoch Jn. Fredk
12 Cheshire Wm. Edwd
14 Savin Thos
16 Drewett Raymond Wm
18 Godwin Wilfred C
20 Mayo Maurice Leslie
22 Doe Wm. Geo
24 Hickman Harry Wm
26 Cooper Mrs
28 Leigh Thos
34 Ginnis Herbt. Wltr
36 Mansell Percy Wm
38 Moody Mrs
40 Davis Arth. Rt
42 Rawlings Geo. Edwd
44 Horton Wm

ROSAMUND ROAD,
Wolvercote.

From 82 Godstow road.
(No thoroughfare.)

1 French Geo
3 Sawyer Leslie Jas
5 Hadland Frank
7 Mailing Thos
9 Tollett Lionel
11 Smith Dawson Felix
13 Eadie Wm. Jn. jun
15 Ward Wm
17 Collett Vernon Victor
19 Lord Ernest Fredk. J
21 Collins Lionel Harold
23 Matthews Frank Chas
25 Dedman Geo
27 Cummings Sidney
29 Ody Albt. Lewis, jun
31 Prince Chas
33 Ward Leslie Arth
35 Coppock Geo
37 Edmonds W. G. David
39 Lyddiast Frank Eric
41 Stone Harry Close
43 Pitts Vernon
45 Hewlett Wm
47 Woodward Edwin H
49 Lane Arth. Stanley
51 Jones Jsph
53 Luxton Fredk. Arth
55 Hillsdon Cecil
57 Rippington Wm. Edwd
59 Sharman Edwd. Chas
61 Sharman Edwd. Leopold
63 Couling Wm
65 Henderson Norman H
67 Morris Rhys Maldwyn
69 Hall Vernon
71 Prince Thos
73 Loveridge Fras. Wm
75 Roach Jn. Hy

East side.

2 Dixey Geo
4 Long Wm. Jsph
6 Hirons Rt. R
8 Hope Sydney
10 Lee Edwd
12 Hutton Mrs.
14 Hiett Edwin Rt. Lewis
16 Lambert Jsph. Cecil
18 Beesley Thos. Edwd
20 Green Thos
22 Bridgman Wm. Risdon
24 Woodford Cecil Ernest
26 Beale Ronald Kenneth
28 Pearce Arth. Hy
30 Jones Edwin Harold
32 Hall Edmund, grocer,
     tobacconist, baker &
     confectioner
34 Allen Jn. Hy
36 Williams Ernest Dudley
38 Maskell Arth. Geo. Wm
40 Gascoyne Jn. Hy
42 Carson Ian Donald
44 Kennedy Edwin Lionel
46 Fleetwood Arth
48 Bateman Ronald Jas
50 Mullen Wm
52 Parker Leslie Norman
54 Gilbert Albt
56 Wilkins Albt. Paul
58 Brown Wm. Geo
60 Crumly Alfd. Wm
62 Hawtin Hy. Rd
64 Phipps Ernest Edwd
66 Neville J
68 Collett Alfd. Claude
70 Adams Evan Leslie
72 Cherry Wltr. Leslie
74 Bowerman Fredk
76 Daines Albt. Edwd

HOME CLOSE,
Wolvercote.

From 104 Godstow road.
(No thoroughfare.)

West side.

1 Neale Jas. Leslie
3 Harper Wltr
5 Tuckwell Geo
7 Preston Edwd. V
9 Warwick Cecil A
11 Roche Jn. Jas. R
13 Sparks Maurice
15 Thornett Geo. Hy
17 Mayo Regnld. Fredk
19 West Stanley H
21 Shayler Jas
23 Oatham Frank B
25 Lock Geo. Edgar
27 Sheppard Wilfred
29 Souch Arth
31 Butt Wallace
33 Knight Fredk. C. R
35 Search Albt. Geo
37 Allen Stephen Wm
39 Churchouse Edwd. Jas
41 Ward Cecil
43 Tutty Rd
45 Davis Chas. Hy
47 Pollard Philip Jn
49 Ensor Geoffrey L
51 Forster Rt. B., D.Sc
     Ph.D

East side.

2 Beane Sydney
4 Taylor Rt
6 Edwards Jn
8 Towersey Cyril H
10 Peart Cecil Frank
12 Harvey Geo
14 Fisher Norman R. C
16 Hind P. Lionel
18 Gaskin Harry
20 Hillsdon Jsph
22 Hillhouse Rt. Winning
24 Heritage Harold
26 Tubb Ernest C
28 Craig Alex
30 Collett Harold E
32 Sanders Geo
34 Foster Regnld. Thos
36 Bidmead Geo
38 Upstone Wm
40 Sanders Saml
42 Philbey Hy. O. M
44 Dunn Frank Sidney
46 Cherry Percy S
48 Stroud Cyril Edwin
50 Boyd Ernest Arth
52 Reed Miss
54 Palmer Hy. Geo. J
56 Summersell Mrs
58 Howarth Geo
60 Lidgett Ivan Frank
62 Conolly Frank B

Acknowledgements

Thanks are due to so many people not acknowledged by name in this book, but without whose help the process would have been considerably more difficult.

Thank you to so many friends and residents of Wolvercote, past and present, who have supported and encouraged me in putting together what are mainly their photographs and memories. Also my appreciation to the many who have provided insights into their personal lives. If memories of a long-ago Wolvercote and it's people are revived and appreciated - then I have succeeded.

One person who I must give especial mention to, is my wife Rita, keeper of my soul. The massive support and encouragement she has given me in the preparation of this book is immeasurable.

Dedicated to all the Wolvercote people who have sent me the photographs and letters in this book, also those who have contacted me by letter or telephone. After all the contents are mainly their memories of a Wolvercote we all loved.

Any profits from the sale of this book will be donated to St Peter's Church, Wolvercote, development fund.

To my knowledge this is the only photograph of brother John and myself with Mother and Father
together. Rex the alsation completes the family, 1936.

Them and Us

Following the publication of my previous book *Growing up in Wolvercote 1931-1951*, I was amazed at not only how quickly it sold out, but also the great interest shown by Wolvercote residents, past and present.

I received letters from Australia, Canada, the United States of America and many parts of Europe, and from far and wide throughout the United Kingdom, in addition I had personal visits, and phone calls were never ending. I was extremely grateful to everyone, but most of all to my wife Rita who never tired of talking to, and entertaining them. I had absolutely no intention of writing a sequel, but circumstances and comments expressed a view, that although Lower Wolvercote was mentioned, not a great deal of information was shown regarding that part of Wolvercote, the reason is quite simple, there really was a 'Them and Us' in those days. I don't mean that it was in the slightest way unfriendly, it was purely one of geographical circumstances, i.e., the canal and railway.

Prior to this visible divide, there was always considered to be a division as early as the 16th Century, this again was more geographical in as much Upper Wolvercote was on higher ground, while Lower Wolvercote was built on what was considered the flood plains (how true that proved to be some 400 years later). There was also what was known as Middle Wolvercote, probably where the railway bridge is now.

Everything remained much the same until 1771, a rural village on the fringe of Port Meadow, the main source of employment being farming on land rented from the Duke of Marlborough. The eleven parishes that formed the City were united which resulted in big changes taking place, one of which was the building of the Oxford Canal due to the need for coal for home and industry. Prior to the time that the Oxford Canal was opened, coal was shipped to London docks, then transported by barges on the Thames to Oxford, a lengthy and costly business. Bearing in mind that the canal was hand dug from the Midlands to Oxford it was a huge undertaking and therefore no surprise that it took almost 31 years to complete at a cost of £310,000. It finally opened in 1790, some 29 years after it was started. Overall it was 91 miles long which worked out at just over £34,000 a mile, a huge sum of money in those days. Considering the number of locks, houses, stables, bridges, wharfs and approach roads etc. that was required, you can truly appreciate the enormity of the undertaking.

Dukes Cut (so called because it was built by the Duke of Marlborough) linked the canal to the Thames, it also provided the route to Wolvercote Paper Mill (owned by the Duke) to supply coal at the rate of over 100 tons a week to fuel the Mills steam engines. The Canal was in effect the thin end of the wedge and created the first landscape division in Wolvercote, which became more geographically permanent with the advent of the railway in 1850. Although Oxford Railway Station opened in 1844 it took another 6 years for the line to continue North.

The Red Lion and White Hart in Lower Wolvercote in 1910 with a very smokey mill chimney in background. (Courtesy Jeremy's Postcards)

Rare view of Wolvercote Paper Mill, 1934. (Courtesy Adrian Gray)

Dukes Cut-off loading area within the Mill, 1934.

With the completion of the line and the construction of the bridge, the physical divide was complete and 'Them and Us' came into existence. This doesn't imply that people became less friendly towards each other, just that personal contact was more arduous, entailing at least a half hour walk. Initially there was a drastic fall in the congregation at St Peter's Church and the time of Matins was advanced half an hour to accommodate the extra time it took Lower Wolvercote residents to walk to Church.

In 1910 the White Hart opened as early as 6 a.m. to cater for the mill workers coming off night shift, their rum and milk was served to them by Harry Drewett (who helped Charlie Cross the landlord out) before going to school. Another early customer was Mr Young who lived in the cottage next door to the White Hart, he ran a small carrier business and would milk his cow and deliver the milk in the early hours (his cottage along with those of his immediate neighbours would be demolished in 1955 to make way for the new entrance for the Paper Mill). Due to the fact that the mills furnaces were coal fired, the black smoke that emerged from the Mill chimney was considered to be a welcome and homely sight to the bargees who delivered it via the canal, to them it signified a well earned rest, not only for them but also their horses who would be stabled behind the pub. The bargees used to say the residents must have webbed feet and referred to Lower Wolvercote as Gander Island. It seems that every weekend when the Mill Wheels stopped turning the village was flooded, to counteract this the Mill built a high bank along the length of the river to contain the water.

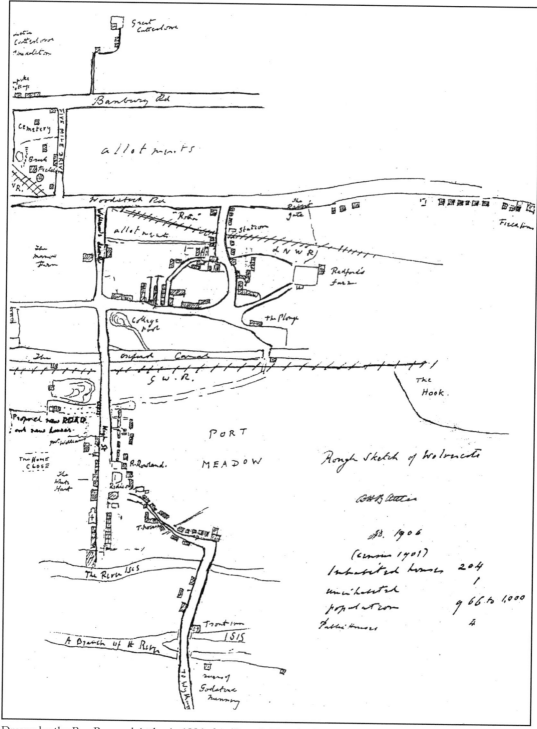

Drawn by the Rev Bernard Attlee in 1906, this 'Rough Sketch of Wolvercote', as he called it, is a beautifully detailed record of early 20th century Wolvercote.

First Turn and Abbey View cottages, 1934.

Betty and father Charles Pratley at doorway of No. 1 First Turn, 1934. (Courtesy James Pratley)

Jane Trott's birthday party - Wolvercote Infants School, 1927. The group includes: Ron Williams, Ron Dawson, Joe Williamson, Joan Belcher, Joyce Smith, Doreen Payne, James Pratley, Doris Couling, Charlie Brown, Iris Mott, Dennis Collett, Betty Pratley, Dorothy Hands, Keith Howard, Phyllis Collett, John Saxton, Phyllis Payne. (Courtesy James Pratley)

Dennis Collett and Betty Pratley. Jane Trott's birthday party, 1927. (Courtesy James Pratley)

Herbert Edmund Stockford (left) with grandson John Austin Stockford, 1928, note Abbey View Cottages in background.

Dorothy Christine Stockford (above) aged 21.

Mother with her father and grandmother, 1928.

Charles Stockford, Freda Coles (mothers sister). ?, ?, mother holding John, Len Stockford, Jack Stockford, parents and godparents at the christening of John A. Stockford, 1928.

Pre 1930 not a great deal of progress took place in the building of private dwellings. This started with a vengeance during the 1930s. Lower Wolvercote had the Red Lion, White Hart and the Baptist Church. Upper Wolvercote, The Plough, St Peter's Church and the School, which as a result of geographical location provided a venue conveniently accessible and didn't involve a strenuous, tiring walk.

As kids in the 1930s, we usually said goodbye to our mates when we came out of school, other than Choir practice on a Mon and Fri, Cubs, Scouts, Brownies or Guides all held in the old Du Merricks farm (later as home for the Boys Club) usually on a Wed, therefore, other than school, we seldom met up socially, the result being that contact between Upper and Lower inhabitants was somewhat restricted, particulary in the winter months, other than sliding on the frozen Gullet we rarely went down there from Upper Wolvercote. Summer was quite different, not only did we meet up along the canal when the fishing season started, we virtually lived there when swimming at either Toll Bridge or the Trout. Another great change that occurred at this time was the considerable re-development that took place. Oxford City council developed the land purchased from the Duke of Marlborough from First Turn as far south as the L.M.S. railway line, this was to conform with the governments nationwide improvement scheme.

Many of the existing houses in Upper Wolvercote were owned by H. O. King. These included Abbey View cottages in First Turn, Westview cottages where Osborn Close is now and Shuffreys Yard, which was reached via a lane at the side of Hobsons Riding stables. All the residents from these cottages were re-housed on the new St Peters Road estate.

Everyone was sorry to see them go as they were rather picturesque and had been occupied in many cases by the same family for generations, what with lack of upkeep and maintenance over many years, all were in a sorry state of disrepair.

St Peters Church viewed from No. 1 First Turn. (Courtesy Jeremy's Postcards)

Shuffrey's Yard - looking east, 1934.

Shuffrey's Yard - looking west, 1934.

Westview cottages - looking east, 1934.

Green Road viewed from railway bridge, 1934.

Northern end of Green Road, 1929. Hobsons Riding Stables were behind the house with the dormer windows. (Courtesy Jeremys Postcards)

Artist's impression of Green Road as it was in 1935.

Water was supplied from a Well, there was no sanitation or electricity and having been friends and neighbours for many years, they didn't take kindly to losing their homes, no more than they did with having strangers as their new neighbours.

Once the emotional shock was replaced by excitement, not to mention the utter joy and convenience, together with the luxury all the modern devices provided (the bathroom being a particular favourite), a flush toilet which replaced a visit to the thunderbox at the bottom of the garden was beyond their wildest dreams. At 5 bob a week they soon adjusted and enjoyed their new found friends and neighbours.

As far as I recollect, none moved into the new houses being built down Lower Wolvercote, they probably couldn't afford the rent. The overall situation was a lot different down there, in as much that the majority of houses being built were private, and could, for the princely sum of 7/6d a week be rented, on

A Mangle, a luxury few could afford, 1934.

Aerial view of Lower Wolvercote prior to being developed (note the paper mill chimney).

the other hand, you were able to purchase them for £395 with a weekly mortgage of 10/6 a week.

Considering that in the mid 1930s this was a third of a weekly wage, it didn't leave much for a family to live on, none the less, the occupants were naturally looked upon as being wealthy, some even owned a mangle, a luxury many could only dream of who were struggling to find 5 bob a week rent. So it was 'Them and Us' became more obvious.

Up to this period the number of houses in Upper Wolvercote was no more than 80. Lower Wolvercote had around 120; their population was more than double and during the second half of the 1930s this would increase threefold to almost 360 houses.

In Upper Wolvercote one of the first new houses to be occupied was Number 27 First Turn, it was one of a pair of 4 semi-detached priced at £395. Noel Sutton bought it, he was earning under £5 a week, it took him years to pay off the mortage with the 'Halifax Building Society'. It sounds like a gift today, but you have to bear in mind you had to lay down 10% deposit and weekly payments were 10/6. With £250 a year considered a good wage their wasn't much difference between mortgage and rent payments. Those who could muster up the deposit became first-time house owners, which also applied to the new occupants of the Lower Wolvercote houses.

With the increase of houses and consequently the population, our shopping habits had no choice other than to change. Apart from Homer Stone at the end of Cyprus Terrace, and Mrs Humphris along The Green, there was nowhere handy to shop. To serve the new estate Cecil Eyres opened First Turn Stores in a shop built by H. O. King.

High Street, Lower Wolvercote 1910, note the horses. (Courtesy Ann Stockford)

Postcard addressed to Charles Stockford. His house on the extreme left of the photograph has '08' on the gable. Viewed from the road the gable to his left has '19' and to his right '09'. (Courtesy Ann Stockford)

Charles Stockford with son Keith, 1918. (Courtesy Ann Stockford)

Wren's Cottage and Meadow View Cottages, 1936.

Wytham viewed from Trout Bridge. (Courtesy Jeremy's Postcards)

Wolvercote Baptist Church, 1905. (Courtesy Gerald Collett)

Harry Robinson and father outside 167 Godstow Road, 1936, note the cordon pear tree. (Courtesy Verona Newbold)

Harry Robinson and his wife proudly pose by their new lorry. (Courtesy Verona Newbold)

No. 167 on right hand side of photograph, 1906. (Courtesy Jeremy's Postcards)

No. 167 on extreme left of photograph, 1906. (Courtesy Jeremy's Postcards)

St Peters Church, Church Road. Wolverote, 1906. (Courtesy Jeremy's Postcards)

William Warmington 3rd from right with sidesmen outside tower door. St Peters Church, 1914. (Courtesy Ann Stockford)

Left: William Warmington, 1911. Right: William Warmington, Churchwarden St Peter's Church, 1914. (Courtesy Ann Stockford).

Bill and Joyce Warmington on their wedding day with part of their cottage (now the Trout Inn) in background, 1928. (Courtesy Ann Stockford)

The Warmington cottage today.

Lower Wolvercote faired somewhat better and were well catered for. At the top end of Elmthorpe Rd you had Maud West opposite Walter Simms on the other corner. A little further along Godstow Rd was Harry Gillett the newsagent, continue along on the same side was Jack Cross for cycle repairs and a haircut (a pudding basin plonked on your head and a quick going over with the clippers, all for a tanner). Beyond the bend in the road past the Red Lion was Chamberlains sweet shop, a short distance past Toll Bridge was a real favourite in Bonds Sweet Shop, attracted inside by the rows of boiled sweets temptingly displayed in glass jars on shelves behind the counter.

Over the Trout Bridge the road ran dead straight to Wytham over a series of little humped-back bridges over the streams, a great favourite with the American troops during the war, showing off in their Jeeps to impress the local girls.

Back to the south side of Godstow Rd (formerly High Street when houses were not numbered) the first shop you came to when you crossed the railway bridge was Wally Allen who sold fruit and veg and was also a coal merchant. He offered a delivery service with his lovely shirehorse and cart. Near neighbours of Wally's were Walter Phipps the vet and Doctor Hoey. Either side of the Baptist Church was Alf Robinson the milkman and Traffords with fruit and veg. Around the corner tempting pears hung from a cordon tree on the gable end of the house of Harry Robinson the coalman.

The furthest-most house in the village was Warmington's cottage (now part of the Trout Inn). Being Churchwarden at St Peter's for many years, he had a long trek to church. Overall Lower Wolvercote was well catered for. With a substantial increase in the population they needed to be! Following the construction of Rosamund Rd and Meadow Prospect all that remains today of Bedford Farm is the house itself, all the outbuildings together with the land was scheduled to be replaced by Home Close. Additional shops were provided by Ralph Bowles with provisions and Post Office, a Butchers shop run by George Gibson & Son, more provisions from Len Beesley who was next door to Vic Surman and his Fish & Chip shop which was enormously popular. Vic, not to be outdone, also ran a delivery service in the form of a trade bike. A friend of my father it provided a good excuse for him to pay regular visits to The Plough, all went well until one evening his wife phoned, when I answered it she said to tell him he had to return home at once 'or else'. By this time Vic was rather the worse for wear and had to be helped onto his bike. With a push to get him going, and cries of "Good luck Vic" he was away. About half an hour later he was back - dripping wet, he said he missed the bridge and pedalled along the right hand side across Goose Green and straight into the cut, we didn't have Fish and Chips delivered for quite a while after that!

The Early Years

Upper Wolvercote didn't fair as well as our neighbours, the only addition we had to cope with our increased population, was First Turn Stores which sold general provisions and newspapers, also the Post Office.

Despite the huge change that was occurring locally, our shopping habits were unchanged regards our main shopping trip to Oxford, which included a weekly visit to Grimbly Hughes in Cornmarket Street, Oxford.

My Father, christened John Walter but always known as Jack, took over the licence of The Plough in 1929 following the death of his father Herbert, who became landlord in 1911 on his retirement from the Oxford City Police Force, which he joined in 1883 at the age of 20, when he became P.C. No. 40.

He had a very successful career and quickly rose to the rank of Inspector. I have a hand written letter he received from Oswald Cole the Chief Constable, dated 10th Feb 1917, following the death of his wife Florence (my grandmother) who died, aged 46 years old on Boxing Day 1916 as a victim of the flu epidemic.
A extract reads:

I am indeed sorry for you in your great loss, it must have been a terrible blow to you after so many happy years together, but something of the sort comes to us all sooner or later. I hope your children are rallying round you in your present trial.

I can quite understand that you feel at the present time you hardly know what to do. Be assured always of my kindest sympathy and willingness to do anything I can.

First Turn Stores, 1946. (Courtesy June Gray, neé Simmonds)

Grimbly Hughes, Cornmarket Street, 1950. (Courtesy Oxford Mail & Times)

The first motorised delivery van used by Grimbly Hughes.

Florence Annie Stockford
(Grandmother) 1914.

Inspector Herbert Edmund Stockford (Grandfather) 1903, seated 4th from left front row. Chief Constable Oswald Cole in the centre on his right.

Inspector Herbert Stockford centre with Morrells employees at South Park, Headington to celebrate J. E. Morrells 21st birthday in 1903.

Inspector Herbert Stockford, umpire, left hand end of 3rd row from the front with Oxford City Police cricket XI, 1904.

My mother and father married at St Philip and St James on the Woodstock Road on the 16th May 1921. Father worked for a insurance company in High Wycombe where they then lived. Every weekend they cycled from there to the Plough and served behind the bar. They would arrive late on a Friday evening and leave after closing time on the Sunday about 10.30 p.m. My grandfather would give father 5 Woodbines as they left. When my grandfather died in 1929 it was assumed to be a natural thing to transfer the licence to my father. Being well acquainted with all the locals from both areas of the village it was a welcome and popular transition. He was one of five children, Herbert, Charles, Elsie, John (known as Jack) and Leonard. Both mother and father were readily accepted and welcomed as the new landlord and his wife by friends and family alike. In those days The Plough had remained unchanged for many years. Just the one bar and a Jug and Bottle, which more than catered for everyone's needs.

Four Stockford brothers, Leonard, Jack, Charles and Bert outside The Plough in 1933.

Left: Dorothy Christine Collier aged 8, with bicycle outside 8A North Parade. Right: Dorothy C. Collier (Mother) in wheelbarrow with the future Gladys Horn, 1904.

St Philip and St James Church, Woodstock Road, 1867.

Left to right: Freda Coles (neé Collier), Fred Hastings, Dorothy Stockford (neé Collier), Elsie Hastings (neé Stockford), Jack Stockford, Chris Collier, Grandmother Collier, 1921.

Leonard Ernest Stockford

1st September 1912, aged 2 years.

1914, aged 4 years.

1917, aged 6 years.

1928, aged 18 years.

Jack Stockford with sister-in-law Win Collier,
outside The Plough, 1938.
(Courtesy Chris Collier)

Five cousins on the
Collier side of the
family outside
The Plough in 1938.
Left to right: Michael
Stockford, John Coles,
John Stockford, Chris
Collier, Ken Collier.
(Courtesy Chris
Collier)

Cutting firewood in
the back garden of
The Plough in 1938.
Jack Stockford, John
Ody and Bill Collier,
Mums father.

Left: Council superintendant and works foreman outside The Plough during installation of main sewer in Wolvercote, 1931. Right: 'Scan', works ganger (who slept in The Plough clubroom throughout the duration of the works), with brother John, 1931.

Players Airman advertisement that hung on the wall of the Jug and Bottle in The Plough, 1938.

Herbert and Charles were employed by Grimbly Hughes in Cornmarket Street. They were joined by their younger brother Leonard on the 21st June 1926 at the age of 16. He was indentured to take out a 3 year apprenticeship in the trade of a Grocer and Provision Dealer with pay as follows:

> 10/- per week for the first year
> 12/6 second year
> 15/- third year

A clause in his indentures stated 'That the Apprentice shall during the said term, weekly on evenings and/or afternoons as arranged as part of the training covenanted for under this indenture REGULARY ATTEND the continuation and technical classes to be held at OXFORD relevant to the Grocery & Provision trade'.

The Certificate of Completion at the end of the Indentures reads: This Apprentice is willing and obliging; and he has carried out his duties to our satisfaction. Signed: J. N. Rogers, Secretary & Accountant.

This is followed by: The council of the Institute of Certified Grocers notes with satisfaction that the within-named term of apprenticeship has been completed by Leonard. E. Stockford, and joins with his employer in wishing him all prosperity and progress in his trade. Signed: Vice-President, W. V. Waite.

My mother did her main shopping at Grimbly's (as it was fondly known), usually on a Tuesday afternoon, I always enjoyed going with her during the school holidays and was fascinated and impressed by those who served her. Everything was sold loose and had to be weighed (i.e., tea, rice, dried fruit etc.), the assistant would scoop it up with a little shovel from a large bag, take a piece of paper that they would form into a cone, weigh it, work the price out in their head, fold the top of the cone over to form a bag, then jot the price down on a piece of paper that would be used after you purchased your last item. With possibly as many as 20 on the list, they would then tot up the total price in a matter of seconds, put the pencil behind their ear, thanked you for your custom before serving the next customer. As you reached the door there was always someone to open it for you who would wish you a "Good Afternoon, thank you for calling".

With no 'settling in' period necessary, both mother and father enjoyed being 'mine hosts'. Being well acquainted with all the locals from both ends of the village it was a easy transition, they, like other members of the family had grown up with them and were readily accepted.

With all the development that was about to take place, The Plough continued to be a popular meeting place. It naturally followed that new faces began to appear at school. This inevitably led to changes which we didn't take kindly to, we were perfectly happy as things were. I sat by Alan (Waggle) Waine, we were good mates, sitting by us on the next desk was John (Chuzzy) Trafford and Roy Phipps (Phippo). Our cosy little space in the corner of the back row was about to be broken up when a bunch of new faces appeared, one extra desk was added to the end of each row, half of the new faces were asked to occupy one chair of each desk by Miss Kear our teacher, to my horror I was asked to stand along with others and occupy a vacant chair. I well remember the name of the boy who I had to share a desk with, even now almost 70 years later I still feel the embarrassment and humiliation I felt over the remarks he made.

The Trafford family from Elmthorpe Road, 1939.
Left to right, back row: John Trafford and Ernest Trafford.
Front row: Beryl, Len, Joyce, Phyliss and Bill. (Courtesy Val Faulkner)

Mother with cousin Doreen, John and Aunt Gert (Bert's wife) 1930.

Mother, John, cousin's Doreen and Cynthia with Aunt Gert and Rex the dog, 1930.

During those days we seemed to have terrible cold winters. The only central heating we were aware of was at either School or in Church. At home we were used to open coal and log fires. As there was a War on, both were hard to come by and in short supply. Sitting by a nice warm fire was a true luxury, the result being, I suffered like so many others with chilblaines, also very painful chapped hands with open sores. My new classmate promptly put his hand up and in a loud voice said 'he wanted to be moved because he didn't want to sit next to this contagious kid'. The result being, I had to stay put, he was moved and Phyllis Jones took his place, together we were appointed milk monitors.

The Woodstock Road roundabout on the newly opened A40. Just two pedestrians looking over Five Mile Drive railway bridge.

The Start of the Thin End of the Wedge

The rural quietness of Elmthorpe Road was shattered in 1935 with the opening of the Northern by-pass, the A40. I had lots of school friends who lived down there. `Skuzzy' Stone, Ron Eadle, Robert MacDonald, 'Chuzzy' Trafford and 'Pickle' Drewett, to name a few. They became aware of the noise the traffic created. Compared to the Western by-pass that followed 26 years later in 1961 it was a mere whisper. This had a far more

Elmthorpe Road under flood water, 1947.

The Drewett family from Elmthorpe Road.
(Courtesy Val Faulkner)

Foden steam lorry, a common sight on the A40 in 1935.

A heavy duty steam lorry, a rarer sight but more exciting due to the masses of steam it created, 1935.

reaching effect, particulary for residents at the lower end of Elmthorpe Road and Home Close, who after the quiet serenity of earlier years adjoining Pixey Mead, now had to endure the continuous thunder of fast moving traffic on the A34, described by many as the road from hell. It was all so horrifically different from the Wolvercote their parents raised them in. With no A40 or A34 as we know it today. The only main road as such was no more than a quiet country road to Woodstock via Williams Lane.

The Canal or Cut as it was affectionally called, was widened and made deeper in 1792, this was to prevent barges becoming stuck as a result of the extra weight when carrying a full load of coal, something that escaped the designers minds during the original construction. Following this, in 1846 the silence was originally disturbed by the construction of the Oxford-Rugby railway line, and the line to Bletchley that followed in 1853. They were the steam trains which travelled at a very sedate speed compared to their successors. The main noise was no more than the gentle 'Chuff Chuff' of the engine, with always a friendly wave from the Driver and Fireman following a blast from the whistle.

Wolvercote Platform, looking north from Godstow Road railway bridge, 1910. (Courtesy Jeremy's Postcards)

Railcar approaching Wolvercote from Oxford, 1919.

L.N.W.R. rail motor car at First Turn Halt in 1919. (Courtesy Mike's Cards)

L.M.S. diesel railcar in Rewley Road station, with the halt gone it did not stop at Wolvercote, 1937.

Horse drawn tram on Woodstock Road, 1901.

Rookery Cottages, Godstow Road, south elevation, 1932. (Courtesy Win Sheppard)

Rookery Cottages, Godstow Road, north elevation, 1932. (Courtesy Win Sheppard)

Harry Waine, long time resident of No. 4 The Rookery, aged 86 in 1947. (Courtesy Oxford Mail & Times)

Harry Waine aged 90, 1953.

Howard Brothers with Rookery Cottages in background, 1922. Back row left to right: Walter aged 12, Bill aged 10. Front row: Ron aged 7, Jack aged 4. (Courtesy David Howard)

Ann Truby on horse adjacent to Rookery Cottages, 1938. (Courtesy Ann Baughan, neé Truby)

Wolvercote was blessed with two train halts, one on the Great Western line called 'The Platform', approached from Godstow Rd. (known as High St), the other was on the London Midland & Scottish line which was on the other side of the Village in First Turn (previously called Church Road), resulting in both halves of the village having good access to the Tu'penny ride into Oxford. Both of these halts were reached by steps—formed by old railway sleepers set into the bank. Taking into account the size of the population in those days, they were well catered for as far as getting into Oxford was concerned, there was also a horse drawn tram available to them from a stop at the Woodstock Rd end of Williams Lane (now Godstow Rd).

Unfortunately, both Halts' were closed in 1926. The Platform was the first to go, followed soon after by the one in First Turn.

Godstow Road was little changed on the south side apart from the loss through fire of Wrens Cottage, and the demolition of Rookery Cottages which were behind numbers 85/87 Godstow Rd.

There were 8 cottages and some stables, Alan Waine lived in one, they were very small inside, one room downstairs and two up, toilet facilities were primitive, they consisted of a wash-house and a privy, reached through an arched opening through the garden wall. Rowland Close now occupies the site, otherwise things look very much the same along this section of Godstow Road.

Not so with Upper Wolvercote where dramatic change was taking place. Du Merricks farmhouse survived, albeit surrounded by St Peters Road estate which occupied the arable land. The farmhouse became the home of the Boys Club and other youth groups, it was only a matter of time before this to was threatened and regretfully demolished. Cyprus Terrace survived, sadly the cottages on the hill and Abbey View cottages didn't, they made way for 4 pair of semi-detached houses.

Osborn Close with it's road surface never adopted to this day by the City Council replaced Westview Cottages and Shufferys Yard. Mere Rd was developed by Knowles & Son the Builders, while somewhat surprisingly Churchill Place survived unscathed.

The 'Unofficial' Mayor of Wolvercote

All of this development had taken place on land owned by H. O. King, who was looked upon as the 'unofficial Mayor of Wolvercote', he was without doubt the most prominent landowner and farmer in the village, his presence was very much felt and respected. He was married in 1886 to Amelia Mott. Osborn was their Grandmothers name, which H. O. adopted as his family's middle name, hence Henry Osborn-King.

The family lived in Church Farm House formerly known as Farm House, before that, The Old Vicarage, although adjacent to St Peter's Church, there are no records to show it ever was. Henry and Amelia had ten children, sadly not all survived infancy.

I remember four of the sons, all professional business men, one of them, William, became mayor of Oxford. Other sons were involved in family business interests. Zacharias, a high class Bespoke Tailors. He was also a Coal Merchant, regretfully, none became involved in the farm. H. O. was a very prominent figure at St Peter's Church where he served as Churchwarden from 1896-1908 in the capacity as Peoples Warden, then again as Vicars Warden from 1916-22, he and his family were very musical. He wrote a alternative tune to the popular Hymn, 'Oh Jesus I have promised', and called it 'Wolvercote'. It became very controversial. In the New English Hymnal it is attributed to the Rev W. H. Ferguson who was the Warden of St Edward's School. H. O. always claimed he had lent him a copy of the tune at his request, when he ultimately claimed it as his. It is said it was never resolved. True or not, it's an interesting story!

He clashed many times with the clergy, perhaps that is why during his life-time he served no less than six incumbents:

1883-89	Rev William M. Richardson
1889-95	Frederick W. Langdon
1895-1901	Walter D. Sargent
1901-09	Bernard H. B. Attlee
	(brother of future Prime Minister, Clement)
1910-27	Edward A. Sydenham
1927-49	Paul E. Rebbeck

Things really began to change for him after the Great War. Being the largest employer in the village next to the Paper Mill, many of his employees failed to return from the conflict. During the War his labour force was made up of German prisoners of war, these were repatriated after the armistice leaving him short staffed, many of his horses were standing idle. With less coal and other goods being transported on the canal, this meant fewer horses were being seen there as well. Animals that we had taken for granted as a everyday sight were fast disappearing.

Henry Osborn-King, 24-1-1857 to 27-1-1942.
(Courtesy Vera Osborn-King)

Church Farmhouse, west elevation, 1910. (Courtesy Vera Osborn-King)

St Peter's Church, west elevation, 1904. (Courtesy Jeremy's Postcards)

St Peter's Church, south elevation, 1904. (Courtesy Jeremy's Postcards)

St Peter's Church, interior, 1904. (Courtesy Jeremy's Postcards)

Shire horses taking a lunch break, 1936.

Returning to the stables after a hard days work, note the lunch basket, 1936.

Dray horses in Morrells Brewery, 1930.

Rev. A. B. Simeon. Warden of St Edward's School funeral cortege, 1928.

Great Western Railway carrier's with a load of Witney blankets, 1920.

Great Western Railway Foden steam lorry, which replaced the use of horses, 1931.

One compensation we enjoyed was the heavy haulage steam lorries which were now a familiar sight on the roads, particularly the new A40.

Steam was also being used in farming with the use of the traction engine, especially during harvest time. Despite the increase in road haulage, the horse was still holding its own with the local deliveries. Morrells delivered the beer to The Plough on a dray hauled by a pair of shire horses. Cyril Edmonds delivered the milk on a horse drawn milk float and Wally Allen delivered his fruit and veg to us on his flat-bed cart, his horse knew exactly where to stop without any orders. Occasionally we saw a horse-drawn hearse. At his stables along Wolvercote Green, and those adjoining Church Farm H. O. King must have had at least 20 or more, mostly standing idle. They were beautiful animals and all responded to their name, their grooms treated them like one of the family. With trade on the decline H. O. like the railway was having a lean time.

One of his biggest customers was the Great Western Railway who's deliveries were mainly done by horse and cart. He had supplied them with hay and feed for over 25 years. In 1930 the unthinkable happened, he lost the contract, things would never be the same again.

He didn't take it sitting down. H. O. had a tendency to write his correspondence in rhyme, business letters were no exception. The following is a letter he wrote to the Superintendent of the Great Western Railway when he lost the contract to supply them with hay. It was kindly given to me by Vera Osborn-King, his sole surviving daughter-in-law. (Note: The letter opposite is written exactly as H. O. King wrote it.)

With none of his sons prepared to take on the farm, and those servicemen who did return from active service after the war taking better paid factory jobs, all proved too much for him to continue and the farm slipped into decline.

He died in 1942 after which the farm took on a air of neglect and inactivity that prevailed until 1947, when along with all subsidiary buildings and 'Scrumpy' Howards beloved orchard, the scene of numerous conflicts and chases, with many a lad feeling the benefit of Scrumpy's riding crop, was gone. Sold at auction for £ 10,000.

With the farm and all subsidiary buildings sold H.O. had bequeathed the remaining family business Zacharias & Co. to his children, the girls opted out, and with their blessing allowed the four sons to take it over, they were. Henry, William, James and Cecil, who was the sole survivor until 'Zac's for Macs' as it was fondly known, closed in 1983.

Kathleen Pratley a Wolvercote girl was the Manager of Zac's for almost 30 years, it was she who gave me a wonderful little booklet first published in 1905 entitled 'Wit & Wisdom by Z & Co' written by H.O.

I have included just a few extracts to whet your appetite.

Wolvercote,
Oxford.
October 22nd 1930

Dear Sir,

Thank you for your letter of October 16th

Since half a century ago,
I first commenced to sell,
To your good company, good hay,
You always used me well.
I laid myself out to supply,
To you my primest hay,
I gain your goodwill, as I thought,
This was the proper way.

Alas, I am now cast aside,
And left to burn or gnaw
My hay supplies, since looked upon
As but a 'man of straw'.
Although I begged to have a chance
To furnish you with hay,
And though I thought I quoted low,
You looked the other way.

Even your horses would object
To live on straw alone;
While other dealers thrive on meat,
I'm left to live on bone.
If I had grown rich by your trade,
I should not now despair,
I cannot live on bread alone,
Or on a cupboard bare.

So if I am discarded from
Your favour, as to hay,
I ask you to deal kindly with
Your 'man of straw' today,
By adding the two bob a ton
Unto the contract price.
Don't pinch the breath quite out of me,
As if screwed in a vice.

          I remain, dear Sir,
            Your obedient servant,
         Sgd: Henry Osborn King

Front and back cover of 'Wit and Wisdom' by Z & Co.

A Dastardly Plot—that failed !

'Twas summer time—the time was prime.
Desipere in loco.
And He and She, instead of tea,
Were sipping—well, not cocoa.
And Kasper's work, was nearly done
And *he* was sipping at "The Sun."

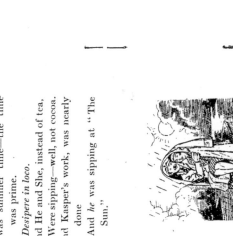

The way was long—the wind was cold.
Thanks to our fickle weather.
And He and She—because not old
Were cuddling close together,
And over them, you'll please to note,
Was shared a WET OFF over-coat.

The Puntsman stood remote from both
Propelling from the stern
The craziest craft e'er seen afloat,
A punt of no concern.
Something had made him very lean
Nor was he noticeably clean.

8

A DASTARDLY PLOT THAT FAILED—Continued.

They journeyed on a league—a league
Well, let us say a mile,
When in his mind grew an intrigue
He smole a ghastly smile.
Thought he, "I'll wreck this blamed old boat
And I'll possess that WET OFF Coat."

This plot being hatched, his mien became
Furtive and ill at ease.
He caught three crabs and to his shame
Shipped several drenching seas.
Youth at the prow, recked not, for they
Were well protected from the spray.

Quoth Angelina to her love—
"Dear Edwin, I've been think-ing
This man's attempt to make us move
Suggests that he's been drink-ing.
This ancient mariner, I fear,
Is too familiar with beer."

Malignantly he pushed the craft
Where piles stood scarce con-cealed,
A rather sharp one caught her aft,
She promptly starboard heeled
And as she swiftly settled down
The demon skipper yelled,
"Now, drown !"

9

A unique way of advertising 'WET OFF' raincoats. (Obviously the work of H. O. King)

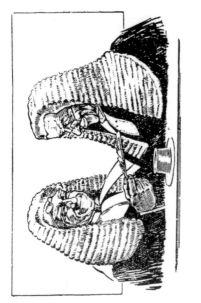

Sound Judgment!

WHAT IS WET OFF ?

The best of judges now aver, " In this decision we concur,
At other raincoats we must scoff, We've well and truly tried WET OFF.
A garment comforting to wear, Distinguished, difficult to tear,
Useful, charming to the sight, Warm, ventilative and light.
No other porous coats will set off Figures or fend rain like WET OFF."

WET OFF IS—

W ELL
OVEN
OOL
ARRANTED
EATHER-PROOF
ITHOUT-RUBBER.

W ILL
ITHSTAND
INTER'S
ORST
EATHER.

ORLD RENOWNED.

*Why wear the coat
we thus describe ?*

**Because it doesn't
rain imbibe.**

I

WATERPROOFS THAT ARE WATERPROOF.

Made and Sold
only
by

ZACHARIAS & CO.

26 & 27 Cornmarket Street

ESTA . OXFORD 1857

Principal : HENRY OSBORN KING

Just two of the eighteen pages in the booklet, each one promoting 'WET OFF' raincoats.

Len and Harry Trafford with H. O. King's Orchard in the background, 1931. (Courtesy Val Faulkner)

Elmthorpe Road, 1910. (Courtesy Val Faulkner)

A Rural Paradise Expands

The quiet appearance that Elmthorpe Road presented in the 1930s is difficult to envisage today. The only vehicle you were ever likely to see there belonged to Albert Trafford who operated his haulage business from number 37. His maroon Bedford lorries were always well presented. The main source of our daily newspapers came from Elmthorpe Road via Patsy Lovegrove for the dailys and magazines. Jack Rance delivered the Oxford Mail on his bike, he only went at one speed — DEAD SLOW.

The yellow bricks which are in evidence throughout North Oxford houses and those used in Elmthorpe Road were produced in T. H. Kingerlee & Sons brickworks at either Five Mile Drive, or from the Quarry on the Woodstock Road opposite Oakthorpe Road, on the site that in latter years became Morris Motors Radiators Branch. Both sites are now attractive lakes. If you get the opportunity to examine these bricks closely, lookout for finger-prints and impressions of a old halfpenny. These were used by the Kiln Workers to assist air to circulate during cooling. I was employed by Kingerlee's for 37 years during my working life, during that time I attempted to find out the history of the brickyards, unfortunately, none existed.

Until the mid 1930s Lower Wolvercote had changed very little since Edward VII was on the throne. On the north side starting with 76 newly constructed houses in Rosamund Road, somewhat surprisingly there were only 21 dwellings from there to the Trout Inn, not including the 15 in Mill Street. On the corresponding south side there was just 40, bringing the total number of houses in Lower Wolvercote to 152.

Private car owners were very few and far between in Wolvercote during the early 1930s, those who ran businesses like my father ran one purely for that purpose, journeys for pleasure were considered a rare treat.

One such car was owned by Neville Rainsley who ran a 1931 Vauxhall which his wife bought him as a wedding present, she was a Boffin of Cooper & Boffin the well known Oxford Bakers. Neville was renowned for his miniature fairground he exhibited at St Giles fair every year, he was also a popular pub sign artist, his work displayed outside many Morrells pubs. He lived in Carey Close when Rita and myself bought a house there in the early 1960s. Shortly after the time of his death his Widow paid me a visit, and offered me the Vauxhall with 27,000 miles on the clock for £365. A sum of money way beyond my reach at that time.

Recently, while visiting a local Steam Rally which included a Vintage car display, there in all it's glory stood Neville's old Vauxhall. On the windscreen was a notice. It read FOR SALE £26,000.

Living as I did in The Plough, it was obvious that home life was so much different than had I lived within a normal home environment. It also provided me with the advantage of amassing a collection of over five thousand cigarette cards which still

Peter Stone, an extraordinary fisherman, 1948.

would not be interrupted by a oncoming barge. Whatever he caught he took home to eat, judging by his success his family must have lived on Perch.

One evening he pulled out a whopper which he decided was too good for the pot, after discussing it with Peter who, having the same adventurous spirit as himself, suggested that he stuffed it, even Arthur admitted that was beyond his capabilities, to which Peter replied "Would you like me to have a go?" an offer that Arthur gratefully accepted. The result was far from professional, Arthurs first reaction was, "We should have eaten it". Little did he realise it then, but he was witnessing the prototype of what transpired to be a very lucrative business. Peter became renowned as a angling taxidermist.

On the same stretch of towpath stood a rather isolated cottage, about half way between the railway bridge and the first drawbridge. On crossing this from the canal you came to the Black Path, it was here that stood Joe White's cottage, if you look really hard you will find evidence of the stone boundary wall that once surrounded it. Adjoining it was a far less imposing residence in the shape of a wooden bungalow, it's last occupants to my knowledge was 'The Black Hat Gang', who lived there during the war years.

They disappeared as suddenly as they arrived. I have no idea who the original occupants were, possibly it was connected with the landing stage that once ran along the bank of the canal at the end of it's garden. Until 1934 it was used by T. H. Kingerlee & Sons to transport the bricks from their brickyard in Five Mile Drive to the Midlands. In between the two drawbridges that were on this stretch of the Canal, was a very boggy field, rarely used for grazing. It was here during the war that George Workman, a Great War veteran (recalled to teach, due to younger men having to enlist) took us to survey the area for a nature study map the school was producing. It sticks in my mind due to the fact that, not only did I enjoy it, but my effort was used by the school for the education project they were involved in, it also whetted my interest in the Building and Construction Industry.

Romany gypsies who frequented the
Black Path, 1934.

A clear view of the boat-turn, half way
between the bridges, 1936.

Irene Collins (nee Ody) with son Michael and friend enjoy a paddle in the entrance to boat-turn, 1939. (Courtesy Michael Collins)

Irene Ody, proud holder of an exemplary school record. (Courtesy Michael Collins)

Typical barge children proudly show off their Sunday best in 1920. (Courtesy British Waterways)

Perce Gardiner lived safely and peacefully in his caravan where you approached the second drawbridge. His only neighbours being from time to time the occasional passing Gypsy, who would possibly stay a week or two. Perce earned his living by making and repairing cricket bats for the university. A peaceful scene that is impossible to envisage today due to the noisy concrete jungle that supports the A34 occupying the area. Adjoining the south side of Godstow Road Railway Bridge, on a area completely clear of shrubs and vegetation was a large irregular shaped natural pond (now known as college pool) that was fed by a shallow winding stream from the cut, known as 'The Feeder'. This in itself collected the quite large volume of water that ran down stone channels that collected the rainwater that entered it from the bridge, then eventually into the feeder. This meandered from the Cut to the Pool, it's depth was governed by the amount of rainwater that ran into it from the stone channels.

As kids we used them for a entirely different purpose. As was the norm in those days we boys wore studded boots, we would go to the top of the channel, place one foot behind the other in it, then slide down. The skill being, that when you reached the bottom you had to leap over the feeder, failure to do so resulted in a good soaking.

Either side of the boat-turn the water was quite shallow making it popular for both paddling and fishing for tiddlers. Apart from the activity that took place in and around the boat-turn with barges. The area to the south of the bridge opposite The Plough was another busy spot. It was here that bargees would 'wait up' before continuing into Oxford, they took the opportunity to catch up with the washing and bathing, hot water would be available from a canal-side fire they would light by the old wharf. While waiting they gave the horse and barge brasses a good polish.

Journey's end for the barges, 1934. Canal basin at New Road, Oxford.

New Street Wharf, coal hand-loaded onto horse and cart sets off for delivery, 1934.

Lower Wolvercote could barely cope with the number of families that descended on the Toll Bridge bathing place during the summer. The bridge was also well known historically. It marked the spot of one of the first aeroplane disasters the country had witnessed. A plaque commemorates the tragedy, not only on the bridge but also in St Peters Church.

To be sure of a space to spread out for a family picnic, it was necessary during the summer season to arrive very early in the day. The area was completely open in those days, no enclosers, which meant picnics had to be guarded against horses who were aware that food was to be had, many a tempting spread was lost !

I should imagine that every kid in the village learnt to swim there. Mr Buckle was the attendant and life guard at the bathing huts. The river along this stretch was quite safe and shallow with the exception of the area on the meadow side of the bridge. This was very much a 'No Go' area, we were always told to keep well clear as there was a whirlpool there which would take us down to kingdom come if we got anywhere near it, we took it as read and kept well clear, fact or fiction, who knows!

Two new additions to the Toll Bridge bathing area to cater for larger crowds, 1954.

Plaque in St Peter's Church commemorating an aeroplane crash in 1912.

The advertised display was cancelled due to the enforcement of an ancient bylaw.

Funeral procession of Lt. Claude A. Bettington and Edward Hotchkiss entering Queen Street via Carfax, 1912.

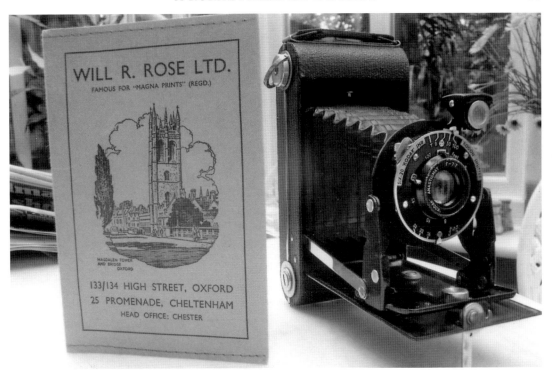

Father's Kodak camera and Will R. Rose folder in which you collected your prints. Having not opened the back of the camera for some 50 years I did so on the 1st July, 2010. Written in my fathers hand was the purchase date, 1st July 1935.

St Edward's School new Boathouse. Note the Toll Bridge, the picture was taken in 1935. (Courtesy Adrain Gray who found it in a shop in Saffron Waldron, Essex)

Toll Bridge bathing hut in 1940. On the right upside down is Justine Butler (nee Holder) brothers Richard is in the middle and Alan on the left. Sister Jean standing behind with cousin Cynthia Day with long plaits.

Brother John and myself enjoying Toll Bridge swimming area, 1936.

The bathing hut surrounded by the 1947 floods.

Ivy and Noel Sutton enjoy a picnic at Toll Bridge, 1947. (Courtesy Bryan Sutton)

Phyllis and Carole Cheshire at Toll Bridge, 1959. (Courtesy Gloria Dunn)

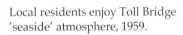

Local residents enjoy Toll Bridge 'seaside' atmosphere, 1959.

Once you became more proficient as a swimmer you would move round in the river towards Scouts Island, so called as it was the summer base of the 29th St Margaret's Sea Scouts. The island is between mainstream Thames and the backwater where we would swim. The water by the meadow bank at this spot was very deep, making it popular to show off your diving skills (more often than not—your lack of them).

The next rung on the ladder was the Trout Bridge. It was here where we really thought we were the 'bees knees' and would dive off the bridge, belly flops were not uncommon

This stretch of the Thames was another favourite, from here we would walk towards King's Lock through Pixey Meadow. A pretty place especially when the cowslips were in season. Once you arrived at the lock you had two choices depending how energetic you felt. Turn left and proceed towards Hagley Pool, then follow the Seacourt Stream back to Wytham. Alternatively, you could cross the lock and wier into Pixey Mead, then onward to Duke's Cut and under the Railway Bridge to the Canal, then either the towpath or Black Path back home.

Myself aged 16 about to dive off the Trout Bridge.

A team of horses assist in tree felling at the Trout Bridge at the beginning of the 20th century.

Gods Wonderful Railway

The Great Western Railway at this section of the line was a really interesting place to be for those like me who were train spotters. Here the lines branched out, either to Worcester and branch off to Lechlade, or the main line to the Midlands. I would spend hours there with only our two dogs, Rhubub and Joe to keep me company, unfortunately this came to a sudden and abrupt end one day. While crossing the field to take up my favourite viewing vantage point, the largest Bull I had ever seen in my life was charging across the field at us.

The dogs took off as if Old Nick himself was after them. I had never seen them move so fast. As for myself I made for the nearest hedge, as soon as I was near enough—took one massive leap and made a undignified landing on the other side leaving the seat of my trousers hanging from the hawthorns as evidence of my achievement.

Every schoolboys dream in those days was to be a engine driver, or at least have a job working on the railway. How, in later years, I envied John Stone who was the only one of us who achieved it, he manned the Signal Box there, not only the excitement that was only experienced in a Signal Box, but the thrill of seeing those superb Great Western steam engines thunder past the open window, plus, you were being paid for it! I was not alone in my enthusiasm for the Railway as a boy, I had the advantage over my contemporaries, as my bedroom window in The Plough was about as close as you could get in the comfort of your own home to the line. It was a vantage point at it's best, with the Signal Box and Siding plumb in front of my window.

I made many friends on the railway, none more-so than John Ody from Lower Wolvercote, he had a large collection of Railway books and wooden Jigsaw puzzles that he willingly let me borrow. I would look at him in awe, he was after all a real live Train Driver! What more could a boy wish for? He would always give me his special whistle as he steamed past. On occasions he would arrange it so he was 'held' at the signal, give me a double special whistle when I would dash across with a jug of ale, climb into the cab and savour the moment.

Another treat was time spent in the Signal Box to deliver a jug of ale. (There was a definite advantage to living in a Pub!) I would relive my fantasies with my own Hornby train set. Together with my brother we had a substantial layout, which in the summer months we ran on the long tables outside the Plough, it also enabled our mates to bring their own trains and run them. Mr Jones from the Signal Box, and many a driver who nipped in for a 'swift half' would join us. It was Frank Hornby who invented Hornby trains, also Meccano, his factory was in Liverpool. Dinky Toys, Bayko, Car and Aeroplane construction kits, also Chemistry and Electronic kits, the list of his wonderful products that thrilled and excited us is endless. Without doubt, the most sought after 'Toys' you could dream of. To further our interest he published a monthly magazine, at 6d a copy, it was a rare treat when we could afford it.

John Stone manning Yarnton Signal Box, 1958. (Courtesy John Stone)

Unusual picturesque Great Western Railway Yarnton Junction Signal Box, 1958. (Courtesy John Stone)

John Ody in the cab of a diesel locomotive in 1962. (Courtesy Michael Collins)

John and Kathleen Ody with daughter Rosalin, 1949. (Courtesy Michael Collins)

A scene to gladden the heart! The 'Fairford Flyer' passes through Wolvercote in 1936. (Courtesy John Stone)

Engine No. 6000, King George V heading north, 1958. (Courtesy John Stone)

Vintage Hornby trains, 1926-31.

Pre- and post-war Hornby, 1937-47.

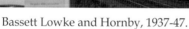

Bassett Lowke and Hornby, 1937-47.   Every boy's 'must have' book, 1937.

My very own Caerphilly Castle, No. 4073.

A scene that sadden's the heart! Wolvercote Signal Box, 1958. (Courtesy Oxford Mail and Times)

After more than a century of faithful service, the siding crane suffered the same undeserved fate in 1963. (Courtesy Oxford Mail and Times)

A Girl's Treasured Memories

All pleasures didn't necessarily cost money, those around us are not only appreciated, but fill us with warm, and happy memories, as remembered in a letter I received from Angela Broadbent who grew up during the 1940s-50s. She paints a beautiful period picture.

I have many happy memories of Wolvercote as a child, when visiting my grandparents, Mr & Mrs Stroudley who lived at 59 Wolvercote Green.

My most vivid memories started after the war when I was about nine years old. Granny had an evacuee during the war but it wasn't until he went back to London that I was able to spend most of my school holidays and weekends with them.

I loved Wolvercote as a child, so different from East Oxford where I lived. I loved the Canal, the Railway and just having the green open space to play.

My Granny was "a good old stick" people would say, she was everybody's friend. I remember watching for the canal boats being pulled by a lovely old horse, and often being led by quite a young lad who seemed to know just how to handle him. I would get quite excited as the boy leading his horse appeared from under Wolvercote canal bridge, because I knew then that the boat would shortly follow, if it were Rose she would moor the boat and make her way across the green to get water from my granny who would also have a few of her freshly baked home-made cakes ready for Rose to give to her many children..

Another regular event was the fair which was held I think twice a year on the green, right outside Granny's house, so you can imagine the excitement we children had, again Grannie was a popular figure with the fair people in those days, she seemed to know every one, so much so that when it was my bedtime it was difficult for me to hide from her, there were too many people that knew me.

I loved Sundays, Granddad always had an Airedale dog so each Sunday whilst Granny cooked the roast lunch, in an oven heated by her coal fire in the living room, Granddad and I would walk the dog, we would walk for miles, all across Drinkwaters' fields, it was wonderful. When we arrived back home, it was my job to fetch Granddad his beer from the Plough, he would give me this large jug which I was instructed to take along to the jug and bottle (this being a type of slide up window from which a head would pop out to ask what was it I needed) for which I had to ask for two pints of light & dark, I didn't know what it was except that it was beer that was usually served by Mrs Pettifer, a large

Granny Stroudley, 1955.
(Courtesy Angela Broadbent)

jolly lady who worked as a barmaid for Mr Stockford the landlord in those days.

When Mum and Dad visited Granny with my younger brother on a Sunday we would all go for a drink at the pub, us children would sit outside with a lemonade and a packet of crisps, feeling really special at having such a treat. There were bench type tables with long seats, where all the Mums also sat whilst their husbands were enjoying a drink inside, it was great and got very busy in those days on a Sunday evening.

I made several friends during my stays at Wolvercote, my best friend was Beatty Savage who lived in ' Ulfgar Road, I can't remember any other names. I did remember the fun and amusement we had spending hours collecting train numbers from the passing trains, and how we would open the gate for people as they came to cross the railway line to Port Meadow to go to the village, most of them to shop.

We would also paddle in the canal, treading carefully over large stones taking care not to fall in, fishing with a jam jar on the end of a piece of string, this would keep us amused for hours. We also enjoyed playing hide and seek in the Dump (this was where the local people dumped their rubbish, the British Legion stands there now) it didn't appear to be smelly, not to us kiddies, there were all sorts of things there, mattresses, sofas, old chairs, tables, you name it, it was there, we would spend hours searching for treasures. I don't remember finding anything worth having, if I had, Granny would have made me take it back.

It was all such good clean fun, my days spent in Wolvercote, are such happy memories, of being a young child to my early teens.

Granny Stroudley sadly passed away in November 1976 aged 85 Granddad five years later in November 1981 aged 90.

The Bill Fallows Era

Bill Fallows our Headmaster at Wolvercote School had strong views on both education and religion, he served as churchwarden at St Peter's Church for 12 years. It was normal for him to start the day at school with prayers at assembly, followed by a reading, invariably from the Old Testament, a favourite of his was ECCLESIASTES, Chapter 1, Verses 1 to 8. Although his Bible would be open, he seldom looked at it as he knew the scriptures by heart. "Remember now thy Creator in the days of thy Youth" etc., etc. Bill would insist the only Holy Bible to use was the Authorised King James Version. Once in our Classroom we would stand behind our desks, Bibles in our hands, waiting for Bill to appear. He would open his Bible and turn the pages for what we well knew he had already selected. There we stood, Bibles at the ready, waiting for his particular choice to be announced, also what format he would adopt, i.e. left to right starting at the front, or right to left, starting at the back, each nervous body waiting to read their verse, "Todays reading, is taken from the Second book of Kings, chapter 18, beginning at the first verse, left to right, starting in the front row," he announced. This was more than a familiar reading to us, you were immediately aware that those of us in the back row were frantically counting, and in hushed tones all were saying, "Whose got verse 27?" much to my relief, I realised it was Ron Eadle sitting on my right. "Whew, that was close". I thought to myself. When the reading reached the end of the row in front of us Ron suddenly put his hand up and shouted out "Please Sir. Please Sir. I feel sick, I need the toilet" and leapt up from his seat. "Very well Eadle, make it snappy," replied Bill. "You rotter Eadle," I said through clenched teeth, as he dashed from the room, hand clasped over his mouth to hide his broad grin. Verse 27, now mine, drew forever closer. I could feel the colour rising to my cheeks, muted tittering could be heard as I rose to my feet. I took a deep breath and began "But Rab-keh said unto them, hath my master sent me to thy master, and to thee, to speak these words, hath he not sent me to the men that sit on the wall . . .", I leave it to you dear reader to look up the end of the verse, unless of course, like me, you have never forgotten it!

Bill strongly encouraged us to take up hobbies, he showed interest and was always eager to hear about the latest products of Frank Hornby, especially Meccano, and the particular project we were in the process of constructing. He also took a interest in all types of sport, both within the confines of school and those outside.

As a boy I was totally unaware of any bullying at school, a subject we sadly hear too much about today. The only incident I can recall that was more of a prank, rather than bullying, took place in the school playground against the railings facing First Turn.

There in the corner was a huge Elm tree, it was just one railing bay away from the

Edith Warmington with Class 1, Wolvercote School, 1904. Irene Ody, 6th from right, front row. (Courtesy Ann Stockford)

Bill Fallows predecessor (E. J. Ellis back row, right) with schools' gardening boy's 1904. Bill Warmington 2nd left back row. (Courtesy Ann Stockford)

fence in front of the Headmasters house, anyone behind the tree was completely hidden from view. About 3 feet away from the tree was a loose railing which could be raised to provide a escape hatch to sneak out from the confines of the playground during breaks, One boy (not the brightest in class) said he was not too keen on the lesson after the break and wished he could miss it. A group of lads nearby told him that could easily be arranged, with that, they promptly took him behind the tree, raised the railing, poked his head through, dropped the railing back into position, and

Irene Ody's Oxfordshire Education Committee medals and bars for being 'never absent - never late', 1904 -09. (Courtesy Michael Collins)

E. J. Ellis with Std VI & VII. Bill Warmington left hand end of back row, 1906. (Courtesy Ann Stockford)

Mrs Slaughter with Std 3, Wolvercote School, 1912. (Courtesy Ann Stockford)

Wolvercote School cricket team with Bill Fallows, 1927. (Courtesy Dina Smith)

Wolvercote School, senior class late 1920s. Norah Howard 4th right front row. (Courtesy Dina Smith)

Bill Fallows with Wolvercote Council School football team in 1928. (Courtesy Dina Smith)

Bill Fallows with athletic team, Wolvercote School, 1928. (Courtesy Dina Smith)

Wolvercote School athletic team 1928. Ivy Pettifer left hand end front row. Ron Cooper left hand end centre row, Bill Fallows on left, Mrs Slaughter on right. (Courtesy Dina Smith)

quickly tied his hands behind his back, then dashed to join up with the rest of the class making there way back to the classroom, where George Robinson was about to take us for Maths. Aware of the vacant desk, he asked where Smith (not his real name) was, receiving a chorus of "Don't know Sir", a pitiful cry of "Help me " could be heard through the open window. It was too much for the majority of the class, who exploded

Wolvercote School infant class late 1920s.

Miss Huckin with junior class Wolvercote School, 1929. Back Row, left to right: Olive Cooper, Flossy Axtell, Glenys Ody, Dolly Viner, Graham Clanfield, Billy Walker, Gwenny Ward, Iris Mott. Middle Row: Miss Huckin, Beryl Clanfield, Rene Collett, Dorothy Hanks, Muriel Jordon, Doris Couling, Charlie Brown, George Pratt, Margaret Bidmead. Front Row: Bert Clements, James Pratley, Jean Allen, Ron Williams, Nellie Loveridge, Beatrice Higgs, Barbara Merry, Joan Drewett, George Stone, Joyce Hastings, John Stone, Violet Carter. (Courtesy Dina Smith)

with laughter. "That's enough" said George (who had absolutely no idea where the cry for help was coming from). "Go and fetch him," with that, up jumped the guilty culprits, not realising that their actions had exposed their guilt!

As punishment, they had a extra hour of Maths instead of Cricket.

Miss Coles with her infant class, in the old Wolvercote School, 1930. (Courtesy Dina Smith)

Headmasters house, First Turn, Wolvercote, 1930. (Courtesy Dina Smith)

Ida Fallows at Wolvercote School House. (Courtesy Dina Smith)

Wolvercote School 1st XI football team, 1948. Back row, left to right: Bill Fallows, Tony Revel, Mick Parker, ?, Dennis Green, Harry Neville, Richard Bayliss, Mr Impey. Second row: Dave Burgess, Tony Pratley, Brian Prince, Archie Prince, Arthur Butler, Colin Chandler, Mick Soden. Front row: Tony Chadwick, ?. (Courtesy Dina Smith)

Wolvercote School girl's second hockey XI, 1948. Back row, left to right: Bill Fallows, Betty Fawdry, ?, Janet Whitehouse, Mary Fawdry, George Robinson. Front row: Vera Eatwell, Shirley Burgess, Pat Flynn, Muriel Viner, Ann Truby, Ann Plato, Mary Smithson. (Courtesy Dina Smith)

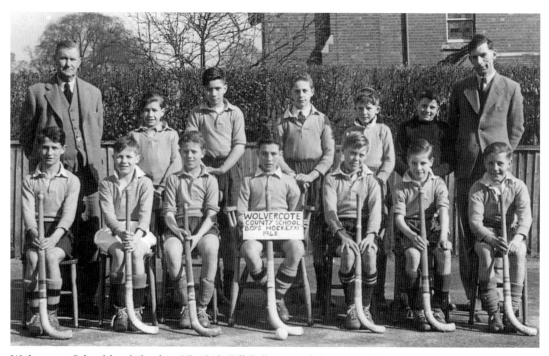

Wolvercote School boy's hockey XI, 1948. Bill Fallows and George Robinson at back. Back row, left to right: Arthur Butler, Brian Harper, Roger Brockell, John Gillett, Richard Gregory. Front Row: David Burgess, Billy Mullins, ? Parker, Brian Prince, ?, Bob Pratley, Keith Plato. (Courtesy Dina Smith)

Wolvercote School girl's hockey XI, 1948. Back row, left to right: Bill Fallows, Mary Smithson, Betty O'Neill, Dawn Sharman, Jean Knight, Sheila Moody, Kathleen Fitzgerald, Pat Payne. Front row: Norma Dewick, Ann Miller, Judy O'Neill, Ann Plato, Betty Smithson, Olwin Witchard. (Courtesy Dina Smith)

Wolvercote School 1948. Bill Fallows and Teacher Mr Impey at back. Boy's include: Fred Drewett, Tony Revell, Arthur Prince, Richard Bayliss, Dennis Green, Brian Harper, Derek Tollet, Nigel Clements, Roy Gascoin, Brian Prince, Arthur Butler, Tony Chadwick, Bob Mayo, Tony Collins, Tony Pratley, Gerald Whitehouse, Colin Chandler, Roger Brockall, David Burgess, Ron Wigley, Bob Walker, Bob Mathews. (Courtesy Dina Smith)

Wolvercote School 1948. Bill Fallows with teacher at back. Girls include: Muriel Viner, Norma Dewick, Ann Truby, Sheila Moody, Dawn Sharman, Mary Sharman, Josie Pettifer, Janet Whitehouse, Jean Knight, Kathleen Fitzgerald, Betty O'Neill, Mary Fawdry, Olwin Witchard, Ann Miller, Judy O'Neill, Ann Plato. (Courtesy Dina Smith)

Wolvercote School Boxing Team, 1948. (Courtesy Dina Smith)

Bill Fallows and Staff, 1948. Back row, left to right: ?, Miss Parker, Mr Robinson, Mr Quarterman, Mr lmpey, ?, ?, ?. Front row: ?, ?, ?, Bill Fallows, Miss Pratt, Mrs Fenner, Miss Coles. (Courtesy Dina Smith)

Anyone entering Wolvercote School in the 1930s could not fail to notice the School Motto above the main door in the corridor, it read:

> For when the one great scorer comes
> To mark against your name,
> He writes—not that you won or lost,
> But how you played the game.

We should always bear that in mind when on the Sports Field Bill Fallows reminded us. He was a real sport enthusiast and always offered encouragement at whatever level. As a result of my previous book I was more than delighted to receive a letter from Bill's granddaughter Dina who lives in Norfolk, Dina's father William was Bill's only son, who I clearly remember being married in St Peters Church during the War, he was a Army Officer and visited his Parents whenever on leave, Bill had every reason to be proud of him. Dina told me that Bill came to Wolvercote from a mixed village school at Cogges. From there he went to Kent where he played football for Deal. He originated from Shropshire and was the youngest of four boys. Tragically his father died a month before he was born. Bill always showed interest in woodwork and did everything he could to help and encourage me when I left school to take up a apprenticeship as a Carpenter and Joiner. I was unaware of his family connections, hence his interest. One brother became a coach builder, another a cabinet maker. Like Bill, his other brother became a teacher. From Kent Bill went to college in London before coming to Oxford, where he stayed until he retired from Wolvercote School. He then returned to his native Shropshire where he died in 1958. He was a great man

Wolvercote Football Club, 1933-4. Outside The Plough. Back row, left to right: Horace Collett, Ron Cox, ?. Third row: Stan Payne, Dan Collett, Rev Paul Rebbeck, ?, Jim Wayne, Sid Collins, Tom Clements, Jack Stockford , Vernon Collett. Second row: Bill Fallows, Cyril Harper, Ron Goodgame, Jack Howard, Frank Davies, Charlie Simms, ?. Front row: Perce Collett, Sid Cook, Perce Ambrose, Arthur Warmington.

who will always be remembered for the help and encouragement he gave to so many young people in their formative years.

One pupil from my generation who really shone at sports was Doug Howse, I cannot think of a single sport or game that he didn't excel in, he was the epitome of sporting excellence, he outshone everyone whatever sport he was involved in, whether Football, Cricket, Snooker or Billiards. When at School or Boys Club, you just knew that if you were in the opposing team to him you were on a hiding to nothing.

Like the rest of us in those days, when you reached your 18th birthday and were not serving a apprenticeship you were liable for a 2-year spell of National Service. Doug reported to Padgate R.A.F. station in Lancashire, his sporting potential was immediately recognised and trained as a P.T.I. (Physical Trainer Instructor) which followed with a posting to R.A.F. Bridgenorth, most of the time he represented the R.A.F. team at whatever sport was in season. Towards the end of his 2 years service, he was given the opportunity of a trial with Wolverhampton Wanderers, at that time one of the top teams in League Football. Doug was successful and offered a contract which he didn't accept, his sole reason being, he wasn't enamoured by Wolverhampton as a place where he would like to live. His Father was furious. His plea for him to reconsider fell on deaf ears. Another good sportsman was Dave Walker from Lower Wolvercote, both he and Doug represented the Oxfordshire County Youth team in 1945. Following this Doug played for Headington United, then back with Dave again they both joined Witney Town in the Hellenic League. Doug is without doubt

Witney Town Football Club, 1951-2. Doug Howse seated 3rd from right in front row. (Courtesy Doug Howse)

Doug Howse receives Player of the Year award plus Hellenic League Cup, Witney Town, 1956-7. (Courtesy Doug Howse)

Doug Howse in centre, Stephen Reiss Club, 1960.
(Courtesy Doug Howse)

one of the finest sportsman that Wolvercote has produced, given the opportunities there are about today it could well have been a very different story. There was certainly something in the family genes that produced good sportsmen as Doug had a cousin, Alf Jefferies, he became a professional footballer and played in goal for Brentford.

The conclusion to be drawn from this, is that Doug was a more than content Wolvercote lad, and no matter how bright the lights were over the hill, home was best. Fame and Fortune? We will never know.

Over the years that followed he achieved huge success in the Billiards and Snooker world. Between 1953-88, a span of 35 years he won no less than 33 Trophies.

He was County Snooker Champion 8 times
     County Billiards Champion 8 times
     Walt Brad Cup Champion 4 times
     Oxford Times Cup Champion 5 times
     Turner Cup Champion once
     A. Cook Cup Champion once
     Sherman Pairs Champion 6 times

John Evans, the County Secretary during this period writes. "It was a fantastic achievement, and I do not believe it will ever be matched."

Doug always gave his best, no matter what sport he was involved in, it wasn't necessarily about winning, it was playing the game.

Bill Fallows would have been justly proud of him, having lived up to the School Motto.

A Taste of Luxury

With the growth in population due to the number of new houses under construction, Morrells was aware of the increase of potential customers and decided to extend facilities at The Plough giving it three bars. The ever popular Public Bar remained, a newly created Bar Parlour where ladies could enjoy a drink (not unheard of but looked down on before the Second World War). Adjoining this was the unbelievable luxury of both Ladies and Gents toilets which were also used by customers from the newly created SALOON BAR, as was boldly etched on the glass panel to the door that divided the two rooms. As they had to enter the Bar Parlour to reach the toilets they were always referred to as "The 'posh uns' from the NOOLAS RAB" which was how the lettering on the glass panel appeared to them on the reverse side.

With the alterations that had taken place on the ground floor, it naturally increased our living space on the first floor. A single bedroom was added and quickly grabbed by my brother John. Another luxury we could all enjoy was a modern bathroom that included a pedestal basin and bath with hot and cold running water and the greatest luxury of all was a flush toilet. Hooray! Another bonus was the bath, no need for the tin bath in the back yard anymore.

Posing by her new Morris 8 Tourer parked outside The Plough public bar, an obvious 'NOOLAS RAB' customer, 1936.

Myself and brother John in our Sunday best in 1936 posing by a Morris 8 Saloon. I can't remember what the occasion was, perhaps a Morris 8 convention!

Bath time in the back yard with mother ensuring John and myself wash behind our ears. At least the sun appears to be shining, 1937.

Considering the effort involved, it's a wonder we ever had a bath at all. To start with my Father would light the fire under the copper. After feeding it with coal for a hour or so the cold water he bucketed in from the cold tap would be hot enough to bucket out and poured into the tin bath, by the time he had finished it wasn't necessary to add any cold. With bathtime over, the whole procedure had to be carried out in reverse, again with the bucket, nothing as convenient as a plug.

The things we take for granted these days, like hot and cold running water, even the humble plug. Flick a switch and you have artificial light, no need to ensure a good stock of candles. It confirms what I have always felt, people in those days were far more content with what they had at their disposal, they didn't have much and therefore didn't expect much. All these new fangled things were viewed with suspicion and mistrust. A treat was an outing of any sort, a visit to the pub being the most common. Anything further afield such as a trip to the seaside was somethimg you could only dream of. Again these were usually arranged by the pub, strangely they were never mixed and were either all male or all female. Like everything else this changed after the war.

Jack Stockford on extreme left with customers from The Plough on outing in 1958, the year he retired. Among the group are Stan Payne, Ivy Bucket, Jack Walker, Mrs Fawdrey, Mabel Pettifer, Mr and Mrs Weston, Joe Pettifer, Mrs Hill, Mrs Castle, Mrs Axtell and George Bidmead.

A Boy's Treasured Memories

I was reminded of this in a letter I received from Allan Waine, or Waggle as he was fondly known. He now lives in Adelaide, Australia having emigrated there in 1969. Although now on the other side of the World, he holds fond memories of Wolvercote during 1930s-60s. In his beautifully descriptive letter, he remembers Sunday night walks to Jacobs Ladder as a real treat, together with other memories of those days. He writes:

I have read an article in the Oxford Mail dated Monday November 3rd 2008 about the response to your book, "Growing up in Wolvercote 1931-1951". I am sure my letter will also come as a surprise, for I have a copy of this book. I now live in Adelaide, South Australia; my name is Allan Waine (nickname Wag or Waggle).

I was in your class at school when George "Dickie" Workman was our Teacher and I sat in the next desk to you, front row, and left hand side.

I must say how much I enjoyed your book as it brought back so many Memories. My sister Ann Truby sent it to me, I also had two brothers Bill Waine and John Truby, the Truby's are my stepfathers' children.

Reading through the book it's amazing how many parallels I had with you.

I was in the choir at Wolvercote church for 6 years under Mrs Dorothy Rebbeck. It was only about a year ago when I heard the news of Ray Venny's death he was a great friend of mine, also his wife Mary who took us on the Choir outings.

My interest in the railway was strong; I used to like collecting train names at the siding. Do you remember a Mr. Gomm who lived in Meadow Prospect? He used to drive the little tank engine delivering goods for the paper mill. I managed to get a ride a few times when he was shunting.

That great train set you had, which you used to set up on garden tables out the front of The Plough, in fact when you eventually sold it my grandfather Henry Waine bought it for me. The big main engine was a Maroon 4-4-2 named Royal Scot.

Going back to our school days at Wolvercote I totally agree with you, Mr Bill Fallows was a great headmaster, strict but very fair, when you got the Cane from him it certainly did hurt.

Another teacher you mentioned, Miss Wren who in fact taught my mother. Some of the other teachers I remember well with great affection are Miss Spencer, Mrs "Granny" Slaughter, Tessie Richards, Mr Robinson, Mr Quarterman and Mrs Boult. Mr Parry, I caught up with him again when I went to Oxford Technical School, St. Ebbe's.

My family and I have been back to visit Oxford 3 times since we emigrated in March 1969. On two of these visits we had 'reunions' at The Plough.

My wife Noreen was a girl from Farmoor, out towards Eynsham. We had 2 girls and 2 boys.

When I left school I also started work at Lucy's Ironworks where I was Apprenticed to Toolmaking, our Foreman was Mr John Hopper. When I finished my apprenticeship I moved up to Osberton Radiators tool room where I worked for 16 years finishing up as Foreman in charge of machining. Then in 1969 we emigrated to Australia.

I retired from work here in 1993, we lived in Adelaide all this time and now we have moved into a retirement village about 70 Kms from Adelaide near the sea.

Referring to some of the characters of Wolvercote, Jack Rance, Scrump (Smokey bush) Howard. We gave him that name when we went down the lane thinking of "scrumping" H.O.s apples, we would look over the wall to see if smoke was coming out of the bushes where he was hiding to catch us. Mr Gardner who made the cricket bats, "Paraffin Ann" who looked after the Horses especially in winter. H. O. King, the unofficial mayor of Wolvercote.

Strange, on reading your book, how we did very similar things like being in the 29th St Margaret's Sea Scouts and enjoying the week camp on Lock island at Godstow messing around in the boats. Fred Garrad was the skipper.

The attachment Wolvercote boys had for the canal was also very strong, as we watched the coal barges through the locks and went fishing there. Sunday night walks in the summer to Yarnton, up Jacobs ladder as we called it, to cross the Railway, have a drink of lemonade at the "Grapes" and a packet of Smith's Crisps, and then walk home.

You mentioned about the arrival of the evacuees, I do remember Margaret Humphries but not Robert MacDonald.

I can also recall the army soldiers arriving on Port Meadow to camp after the terrible defeat at Dunkirk.

Allan Waine, 1946.

The swimming in the river at Toll bridge with Mr Buckle the bathing hut attendant. Also down by the Trout bridge, swim over to the island and sit on the Big Lion until we were chased off.

Since coming here in 1969 we have had a few visitors from Wolvercote.

My mother in 1973, my sister-in-law, my elder brother (Bill Waine) and his wife, Joe O'Neil and his wife, Margaret Dorrill and Fred (Beefy) Drewett, his wife and daughter, they came and stayed with us for 4 days after visiting his younger brother Richard (Dickie) Drewett in Sydney.

Several other Wolvercote people you may have known Eddy Edmonds from Rosamund Road lives in Sydney, Roy Beardsley who lived next door to your mate Albert Collett he is in Tasmania. Jean Cornish is here in Adelaide and Rex Smith who was in the choir with us singing tenor but I lost contact with him.

Well Michael I will sign off here, congratulations once again on your book, when you look back to our school days and growing up I think we were very lucky to have been born and raised in Wolvercote (and I still miss it) although we as a Family are very happy here in Adelaide now with 9 grandchildren and come April we will have 2 great grandchildren.

Adolescent Years

We had a teacher who was affectionately called Granny Slaughter, I doubt if she was 40 years old. One subject she came down hard on us was English. "I intend to teach you the Kings English" she once said. "NOT the appalling Wolvercote version which you children insist on speaking." She then proceeded to tell us there were such things as vowels, which we totally ignored, a habit she was determined to break us of. One by one we had to stand up and repeat chosen sentences, it was hilarious, the more she tried to improve our speech, the more we spoke badly. A few examples being, 'Isn't it', became 'en it', 'Doesn't it' was 'dun it', 'Won't it' was 'wun it', 'Can't it' was 'can it', For 'Hello', we always said 'Wotcher'. "Your misuse of the English language, drives me to total despair" she concluded. She knew when she 'wus' beat.

With the outbreak of the Second World War on 3rd September 1939 came the threat of Air Raids in London. We were issued with Gas Masks and given shelter drill on how to react as and when the siren sounded. Air-raid shelters were constructed at the bottom of the playing fields and parallel to St Peter's Road. It was nothing short of organised chaos which provided us with the opportunity to behave a lot worse than usual. Mass evacuation was taking place from areas that were under threat from air raids, London was top of the list. On the day war was declared evacuees arrived in Wolvercote and were assembled outside the Church to be allocated to local families by the billeting officer. It must have been truly awful for them having not only to leave their homes and families, but also familiar surroundings. Depending on accommodation available to them resulted in even brothers or sisters being separated.

You can well imagine the upheaval caused, not only to families that took them in, but also school. The first few weeks were chaotic, extra desks were brought in, additional teaching staff recruited from those who were retired.

A major bonus to us was, due to the extra pupils, lack of staff and space which resulted in us only being taught for half a day each day. Any thoughts we had regards doing our own thing was soon dispelled.

There were allotments running parallel to the railway line in Mere Road. With 'Dig for Victory' posters everywhere, bang went our half days off. Mornings one week – afternoons the next when we were marched off to do 'our bit '. I can't say that we were very conscientious, the result of our labour was described as 'A very poor harvest'.

It was decided that along with the newcomers, we would all have to have a full medical examination. I have nightmarish memories of, as a 9 year old, being held in a dentists chair while he worked a treadle up and down with his foot and drilled one of my teeth. Depending at what rate his leg went up and down was reflected on the speed of the drill, after 5 minutes or so that was very slow, need I say more?

A short while after that it was necessary for me to pay another visit to the dentist. My Father said there was a good one in Kingston Road, "I'll make an appointment for you" he said, warning me at the same time, that he liked a drop of whisky. I arrived

Albert Morgan with Joe and Rhubub outside The Plough. Albert epitomized the bar customers, they were the salt of the earth. Alberts daughter Rosie, gave me the photo which she has carried in her purse for over 50 years, it was I who took it one Sunday evening in 1947.

A chat over the garden gate, 1939 style (Courtesy Imperial War Museum)

at the surgery about noon on a Saturday, as soon as he bent over me in the chair to carry out a examination, I could smell whisky on his breath. Some five minutes after, he proceeded to pull the tooth out. To say it hurt like hell is a understatement. Holding it up aloft in his forceps, he said "Sorry kid I've got the wrong one, lets have another go." I regret to say the procedure was repeated, "you carry on at this rate I won't have any teeth left, can't you push them back in," I pleaded with him. To my relief it was third time lucky. On arriving home Aunt Mabel (Mrs Pettifer) had sausage and mash waiting for me. To this day whenever I eat it I am reminded of a visit to the dentist that I would prefer to forget!

Prior to the early part of the 15th century there was no consecrated burial ground in Wolvercote. It was what was known as a chapel of St Peter-in-the-East which meant that anyone who died in Wolvercote had to be buried there. So it was, that in 1414 the church was built on it's present site. Not the familiar much loved St Peter's we see today, this was built in 1859-60 at a cost of £1,997-3-1d. All that remains of the original building is the tower which originates from the 14th century, it was rebuilt in the 15th century with part of the original preserved. Its true history is uncertain, but it is evident that old and varied stone was used in the tower we see today. Another interesting relic from the past are the sundial arms (called gnomons), also an inscription 'Redeem The Time', again the significance is unknown. Little was I aware that in later years I would become so involved with it!

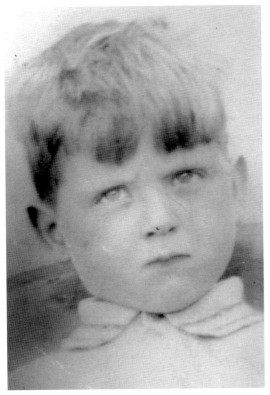

Michael. H. Stockford, 1934 aged 3, the year
I started Sunday school and infant school.

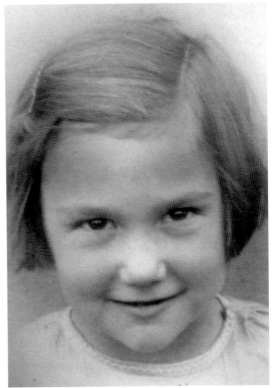

Rita J. Wickens, 1934 aged 3.

Rita and John Martin both aged 3, who were chosen from Summertown Infant's School to present a
bouquet to the Duchess of Marlborough, who opened the Christmas Bazaar at Summertown Church Hall
in 1934. Rev. Canon Evan G. Burrough looks on approvingly. (Courtesy John Martin)

St Peters Church has played a huge part in my life, the memories and friends I have met and shared so much with goes back to early childhood. Sunday School with Mrs Smith and Mrs Tollet at 3 o'clock in the afternoon. Choir practice twice a week under Mrs Rebbecks eagle gaze. Boys from the village as a whole were in the choir (there was always a waiting list). When your voice broke you were encouraged to take on other duties such as being a Server and assisting the Vicar during Sunday services, after a twelve month probationary period of weekday services!

A second option was to become a bell ringer. I took the first option, my brother the second. All was going well until one evening he came home from church after bell ringing prior to Sunday evensong. He was as white as a sheet "Whatever's wrong" I asked him, it took some time before he was able to tell me "Bill Herring was ringing his usual bell next to me when he just collapsed and died" he said. He was 57. Brother John's interest sharply wained, being the right age and attracted to the Army Cadets he chanced his luck with them. As for myself, I took the other road and became a server.

A faithful servant of St Peters from those days with whom I have maintained contact is Bill Crumly, during a recent conversation with him the name of Bryan Sutton came up. It really was a 'Blast from the past'. Bryan lived with his parents at 27 First Turn. Having obtained his address from Bill I wrote to him, the result was most rewarding, not only some photographs that I have included in this book, but also the charming letter that accompanied it from Canada where he now lives. It paints a graphic picture of Wolvercote during the war and early post-war years, even a mention of 'Them and Us'.

Bryan writes:

I was born in October 1936 at Watlington Hospital; as, at that time, my parents were renting in Great Milton. They bought 27 First Turn in (probably) 1939. As my dad said it was as well because the war was soon to stop building.

My memories of the early days of the war are pretty thin, of course. Oxford did not get bombed, thank goodness. I sort of remember some of the soldiers evacuated from Dunkirk, who were camped out on Port Meadow, stopping to talk to my Mother and me and giving me some French centime pieces. Also, my mother was involved in the Women's Institute and she took me out to a project where they built an outdoor fireplace and cooked on it, ready for the collapse of all facilities. I only remember the sandwiches that were served, a chocolate type filling.

My main memories of the war were of queuing. My mother would always take me shopping as baby sitters were scarce, and it was a procession from one long queue to another. Oliver & Gurden's factory outlet in Summertown was one that stuck in my mind. I remember Mum talking about one of the women in the Co-op whose husband had been in the army in Hong Kong or Singapore and who was still waiting to hear that he had survived - I don't think she ever got the news she was hoping for, those long years.

Mum became a fire warden and told me she would sit under the dining room table with a brass fruit bowl on her head when the siren went off. Dad, a tool and die maker, later said he was working twelve hours a day, seven days a week at Radiators making tools for aircraft. In between he was busy growing as much food as he could - the back lawn was dug up for potatoes. One potato he said was so large he took it into work and raffled it — proceeds for the Spitfire Fund. After the invasion scare when they rang the church bells (I read that was in September 1940) he joined the Home Guard. I know he mentioned one exercise on the North Oxford golf course; there was a 'German' machine-gun post and the officer in charge said "fix bayonets, charge"! In later conversations it became apparent that the Home Guard did useful work in guarding sensitive areas; the grain store at Kidlington and a research area in the University where an engine under test was being run.

Neville Rainsley's Smallest Show on Earth, 1935. It can be seen today in the Museum of Oxford in the Town Hall.

To a large extent we were sheltered from the war. Long after it was over, I was standing with a friend in Cornmarket waiting for a Number 4 bus and there was Neville Rainsley. He lived up in Fire Mile Drive, before the war he had exhibited fair ground models at a booth at St Giles' Fair ; during the war he worked at Radiators with my father. This was common, many men who had not worked in factories were directed to such work if they were too old or not fit for the armed forces and Dad made friends with many of them who in happier days had been musicians or artists or whatever. Anyway, at the time I was working in Portsmouth, and Neville said "I was there for two weeks during the war". I knew that Neville had been with the Auxiliary Fire Service during the war, and the thought that the bombing had been severe enough for men and pumps to drive the sixty miles and stay for two weeks saddened me. A next door neighbour, Stella Taylor, once mentioned that just out of school she had been one of the girls who directed by radio the pilots of the Battle of Britain and "heard them die".

At the back of number 27 was the 'Estate' a development of Council Houses, subsidized housing, due to the snobbery of the time I was not encouraged to mix with those children. To my mind this is the down side of the time, which was a very safe time in many ways. In the same way my father always drank in the Saloon bar of the Plough rather than the Public Bar, hence I have no great memory of the Aunt Sally games that went on at the front - very much an Oxfordshire tradition. I remember seeing the wall that had been built at Cutteslowe to segregate the Council Houses from the upper middle class houses - fortunately it was eventually demolished. But I did have some friendships with the local children. I do remember going with Mike Brown to pay his grandmother's rent. She lived in one of the cottages in Church Lane, backing on to the Saxton's small holding. We went into H. O. King's bailiff's office, upstairs in the building on the left of the big gates to his yard. Round the yard were the wagon sheds. In the office was the bailiff at a high desk on a high stool. The building is now a private house and the spinney that faced the row of houses of which 27 was one is now a block of flats. It used to have red squirrels and we used to watch them until the grey squirrels took over.

The garden was one of my father's loves. Apparently it took a lot to get into order. He was always burning weeds on the bonfire, and said that his father had come over from High Wycombe to dig out the bindweed with a process of double digging, where a second spadeful was taken out onto the first. Before the war he had bought a wooden

Terry Saxton who lived in Church Lane with Bryan Sutton and Bob Soden, who's father was a chimney sweep. Bryan became friends with him after his father who attempted to sweep his own chimney, unscrewed the brush the wrong way, causing it to become stuck. He called Mr Soden in to retrieve it - he never attempted to sweep his own chimney again.

Bryan Sutton outside 27 First Turn with his 10-speed bike, 1951. (Courtesy Bryan Sutton)

of the weekend we pulled it back. That was the great part of those days, there was so little traffic and we were comparatively safe. The only adult supervision was the curator of Youlbury, who also ran the tuck shop. In later years the scouts raised money by having whist drives in the village hall. Even later came Bob-a-Job Week where scouts went door-to-door offering to do some job for a shilling. I found it a good experience as we were offered some interesting jobs and given instruction.

In a very complicated way the Scouts were very significant for me. There was a Scouting program on Radio Luxembourg every Saturday morning. I asked Dad if I could listen to it and he said that it was his radio (the only one in the house) and nobody was going to listen to Radio Luxembourg (which was notorious for broadcasting very popular music) on it. So I decided to build my own. I scrounged some earphones, wound a coil round a piece of broomstick, bought a crystal at Westwoods in George Street and built a crystal set. This led to a hobby of electronics, helped by the physics master at school and others, and eventuality to an apprenticeship in electrical engineering and a career that led me through most of Canada.

One difference between those days and now is how little we had. Books we borrowed from the library. If anything broke it got mended. This was not just because of the war, it was a major part of the way of life. All tools were hand-operated. The soldering iron had to be heated in the fire or on a primus stove. Though the war did add to the need to improvise. Dad had played the flute for many years: during the war it was impossible to buy the pads and replace broken springs - I remember him making pads and trying sausage skins for a covering, also making springs from sewing needles and hardening and tempering them on the electric cooker.

1947 was significant for me in a very different way. The new Education Act set up the 11 plus examinations where a percentage of the Council School children were to go to the local grammar school. I was lucky and went off to the City of Oxford High School in George Street. This could mean eligibility for a college degree. In fact, though I stayed on into the sixth form my marks were not such that I could get into a University, and anyway my family could not have afforded the costs involved. However, I was eligible for an apprenticeship with GEC in Coventry. A five year apprenticeship, with enough pay to cover accommodation with a bit left over. Two and a half years of the five being full time education at Birmingham College of Advanced Technology leading to the equivalent of a degree, the other two and a half years being a term in each department of the company. It was a wonderful scheme and I am sad that it was dropped in latter years.

However, I am talking of my time in Wolvercote. To some extent I changed my way of life, school in Oxford meant a change in friends. If the idea of the 11 plus was to democratise education I am not sure that it did. At the High School we all seemed to be of a common social class, sort of upper working class. The education was excellent, though I personally found the attitude of many of the masters rather authoritarian. Homework became a fact of life, two or three hours a night was common for me - not a fast learner. I continued with the Scouts every Wednesday up until the time I left for Coventry, and went to pretty well every camp.

Towards the end of my time at the High School I got into cycle touring, staying at Youth Hostels. At that time it was an extensive network, charging I think 2/6 for a night's accommodation in dormitories. One summer I took my 10-speed up to the Godstow Road roundabout and hitch-hiked with it heading North for Scotland. Several lorry rides took me up into Lancashire, at that time a seventeen year old was fairly safe hitch-hiking, and the lorry drivers were a fine group of people. I stayed at the hostel just outside Todmorden and as I cycled up to it I passed the mill workers coming out and still remember the distinctive sound of their clogs on the pavement. I also encountered the granite sets of the roadway, not too good with the narrow high pressure tyres of my bike. In two weeks I cycled round the Southern part of Scotland, up Loch Lomond and as far North as Inverness.

For me, Wolvercote and growing up there, hold warm and happy memories.

Lest We Forget

One only has to look at the names on the War Memorial in St Peters churchyard to appreciate the sacrifice that Wolvercote alone made, so many families were ruined forever, none more than the Loveridge family. With a total of 5 sons who enlisted in the army, and serving in France, in a space of just 4 weeks Albert and George (who was just 19) were killed in action. Thomas was seriously wounded and subsequently died of his wounds. Fredrick and Alfred were also wounded but thankfully recovered. Fredrick was awarded the silver war badge and certificate for his courage, his wounds were considered to be serious enough to warrant him being discharged on 27th May 1918 as unfit for active duty, he was awarded a pension of 27/6d a week for 4 weeks, this was reduced to 16/6d a week to be reviewed every 52 weeks. Due to the severity of his wounds, he was in and out of Hospital until 1924, when on 9th May as a result of them, he died. To give just one more example of the pension awarded, and the hardship endured by the family, was that of Edmund Cox. He was employed as a Porter by the Great Western Railway. Having obtained their written permission, he enlisted at the age of 30 yrs 9 months on the 20th April 1915 into 200 Regiment, Royal Garrison Artillery. After 4 weeks training he was posted to the front line, leaving behind his wife and 1 yr old daughter Beulia. Just over 1 year later, on 6th June 1916 he was killed in action. His widow received 19/3d a week pension.

Three other names on the Memorial from the same family is that of Waine: Walter, Frank and Albert. The Loveridge brothers and Albert Waine were cousins to Frank Waine. Walters sister Elizabeth Loveridge (nee Waine) was Albert, Thomas and George Loveridge's mother, she was married to Absolem, had 15 children who all lived in Wolvercote. Frank Waine who was in the Oxford & Bucks, was killed in action on 14th May 1916. Walter Waine who was in the Royal Engineers, was killed in action on 22nd June 1917, he was 49 years old, before the war he was employed by H. O. King.

Unite the number of these two families together and the grief they had to bear with the hardship, must have been intolerable.

As far back as my memory takes me I was more than aware of Armistice day on November 11th each year, and have always been conscious of it's significance. With the exception of Edward Miller who was killed in the Korean War in 1951, the other 52 names on the War Memorial are those killed in the Great War 1914-18.

Inside the church is a plaque with a further 25 names of those who were killed in the Second World War 1939-45. These names are all Wolvercote men. In contrast, just 50% of those in the 1939-45 conflict were local men the others arrived in the parish in the 1930s.

St Giles in 1914, the only vehicle being a horse-drawn tram.

Cornmarket Street, 1914.

Wedding day photo of the marriage of Violet Waine to Edwin Dear taken on 14th February 1914 in the back garden of 50 Elmthorpe Road. Back row, left to right: ?, Sidney Waine, Ernest Waine, Percival Dear, ?, Albert Waine. Middle row: Baby ?, ?, Mary Ann Waine (nee Stroud), Violet Waine (Bride), Edwin Dear (Groom), Susan Dear, ?. Front row: ?, ?, Florence Dear, Dorothy Waine, Florence Waine. (Courtesy Maureen Waine)

Propaganda
Poster, 1914.

Colour Sergeant recruiting in Broad Street, 1914. (Courtesy Oxford Mail & Times)

Wolvercote lads who answered the call, 1915. Oxford & Bucks Light Infantry, 4th Reserve Battalion, 262 Infantry Battalion. Front row, left to right: ?, Frank Collett, Jack Stockford, Harry Drewett, ?, ?.

Owen Price, extreme right, killed in action in France in 1916. (Courtesy Gerald Collett)

Left: Frank Collett, Oxford & Bucks Light Infantry, 1915. (Courtesy Les Collett)
Right: A recruitment advert of a relaxed and smiling 'Tommy' encouraging them to 'Sign Up'.

Left: John Walter Stockford aged 16, 20th January 1916, 10th Battalion, Oxford & Bucks Light Infantry. Right: Bugle Major Charles Pratley, 43rd Battalion, Oxford & Bucks Light Infantry, 1914. (Courtesy James Pratley)

Left: Dorothy Christine Collier (later Stockford) aged 19, 4th August 1916. Above: Maud Aldridge (later Pratley) aged 19, 1916. (Courtesy Kathleen Pratley)

Jack Stockford, Edith Warmington, Charles Stockford, 1915. (Courtesy Ann Stockford)

Dorothy Collier wearing spare uniform belonging to her brother Chris on right. With their father William in the middle, 1916. (Courtesy Chris Collier)

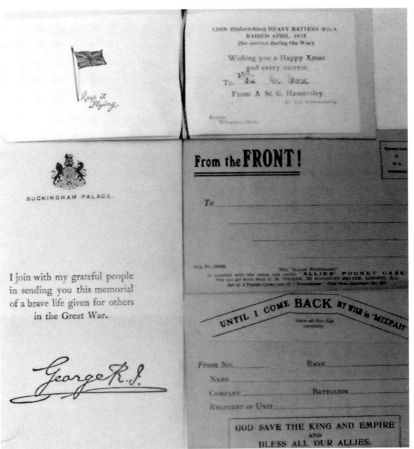

Christmas card from
The Front from
Edmund Cox, 1915.
(Courtesy Gill Harper)

Edmund Cox. No. 200
Regt. 128th Royal
Garrison Artillery,
killed in action, 1917.
(Courtesy Gill Harper)

A wonderful photo of Trooper Edmund Cox with
horses in 1916. (Courtesy Gill Harper)

Tune—"March of the Men of Harlech."

(The second four lines, remember, are the same tune as the first four.)

Men of Britain march together !
Fearing neither foe nor weather,
Lift your feet, don't waste your leather,
  March along like men !
In this war we'll march for miles,
Face the music, bear the trials;
Beat the foe with all his wiles,
  Beard him in his den !

  March ! The guns are calling !
  March ! Brave men are falling !
  March right on with cheer and song
  No dangers us appalling.
  Victory we'll win together,
  Navy, Army, Airmen, Terrier;
  From the foe we'll turn back never,
  We shall win ere long.

For the Empire we are fighting !
Wrongs 'gainst others we are righting!
All for King and Home uniting,
  We now march along.
When our thoughts go homeward turning,
When true hearts for us are yearning,
When within us love is burning,
  All this makes us strong.

  Though from food we're fasting,
  Though with thirst we're parching,
  Strong of will, we'll climb the hill
  Though feet grow sore with marching,
  One and all we'll march together,
  'Cross the slough or through the heather ;
  Fight the foe, far he shall never
  Curse the world again.

                      H. F. Morris.

belongs to :—

No.

Name

Unit

THE ALLIES POCKET CASE

Home Address :

GOD SAVE THE KING!
AND
KEEP THE OWNER SAFELY.

HEAVENLY FATHER, my heart is full of gratitude to Thee for past care of me; and of those whom I love. Keep us all while we are separated from each other; as Thou only can'st. Shield us in danger's hour. Forgive all that has grieved Thee, or injured others, in the past life; My trust is in Thee! Hear my prayer for Comrades in this great war, incline their hearts to think of Thee. Keep the Officers who lead us; help us all to render them cheerful obedience. May we all endure hardness, as good soldiers of Jesus Christ. When suffering or death comes to us, may the Holy Comforter be as a friend at our side. Grant us speedy Victory over our Enemies; if it be Thy Will. God save the King, the Queen, and all the Royal Family. Give wisdom and courage to all who control the affairs of our Empire. Bless all our Allies, and save them and us with Thy Great Salvation ; through Jesus Christ Our Lord. Amen.

Tune—"Eternal Father, Strong to Save."

Lord God of Battles! Lend Thine aid!
  Put out for us Thy Power and Skill ;
With Thee to help, we're not afraid;
  But forth will go, it is Thy Will.
    Be with us through War's awful fray
    Lord give us Victory, we pray !

We sought not war—we dwelt in peace
  Till wrong was done, across the wave
Thou saw'st our foes, their arms increase,
  Whilst they the hand of friendship gave.
    Now hearts of Britons pray to Thee
    Who made us great, Lord keep us free !

Great Guardian, keep the friends we love,
  Our King, our Allies, all who fight ;
Guide by Thy Council from above,
  The plan of this Campaign for Right;
    Lord God of Battles wield Thy sword;
    WE TRUST IN THEE FOR
    VICTORY, LORD! Amen.

                      H. F. Morris.

The King graciously accepted these verses.

This useful Pocket Case was designed, and words composed by:

Published by:
G. E. Wright (Printer),
36, Finsbury Square.

The 'Allies Pocket Case' issued to Trooper Edmund Cox, 1915. (Courtesy Gill Harper)

Gv R1

H E whom this scroll commemorates was numbered among those who, at the call of King and Country, left all that was dear to them, endured hardness, faced danger, and finally passed out of the sight of men by the path of duty and self-sacrifice, giving up their own lives that others might live in freedom. Let those who come after see to it that his name be not forgotten.

Gnr. Edmund Cox
Royal Garrison Artillery

Scroll sent to the widow of Edmund Cox from King George V in 1917, also a commemorative bronze plaque. (Courtesy Gill Harper)

Above: Arthur Henry Drewett, 2nd/1st Bucks Battalion Oxford & Bucks Light Infantry, killed in action 22nd August 1917, aged 38. (Courtesy Val Faulkner)
Right: Fred Loveridge, Oxford & Bucks Light Infantry, 1917. (Courtesy Gill Harper)

Left: George Loveridge, Royal Engineers, 1915. Right: Tom Loveridge, Oxford & Bucks Light Infantry, killed in action, 1915. (Courtesy Gill Harper)

Charles Tovey, Royal Garrison Artillery, February 26th 1916, killed in action, 1917. A message on the back of the card reads: 'My darling Nellie, Would that I would bring this card instead of sending it. But I have kissed it, and know you will too my darling.' (Courtesy Ann Stockford)

Albert Loveridge, Royal Engineers, 1915. (Courtesy Gill Harper)

Left: Frank Waine, No. 2379, Oxford & Bucks Light Infantry, killed in action, 14th May 1916. Right: Walter Waine, No. 125203, Royal Engineers, killed in action 22nd June 1917, aged 49. (Courtesy Maureen Evans)

Left: Bill Warmington, Royal Garrison Artillery, 1915. Above: Charles Warmington, Royal Garrison Artillery, 1915. Right: Nellie Warmington (later Tovey) 12th June 1915. (Courtesy Ann Stockford)

Left: An example of how the horrors they were to encounter was glamourised with the ladies urging them to 'GO'. Right: the obverse view of the postcard below.

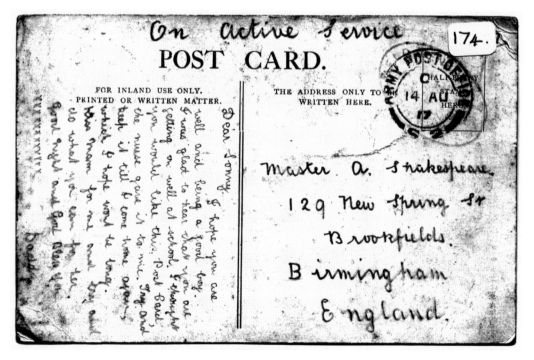

A postcard sent from the front, 1917.

"I always wash my pussy in scented soap."

A very risqué postcard sent from a soldier, about to leave for the Front, dated the 7th January 1917. He is serving in the 3rd Rifle Brigade. He writes: Dear Brother. We are leaving here tonight for the Front. I hope you received my letter safely. Remember me to all the boys. So Goodbye and God Bless. I remain your loving brother Matt xxxx. P.S. look out for my name on the lists!

Sadly so many men were attracted by the glamour and adventure this poster offered - never to return.

A photograph Rita's Grandmother Lucy Harris had taken at a studio, at the request of her husband who was serving at the front.
Left to right: standing; Gladys (Rita's mother) and Gertrude. Seated: Arthur, Violet by her mother, 1916.

A Christmas card received by 11-year-old Gladys Harris in 1916, from a L/Cpl. A. Pusey No. 5259 20th Hussars, No. 1 Remount Base, Rouen.
Dear Friend. Just a few lines to let you know I am one of the receivers of the many scarfs that were sent out from your school, and it was your name on the scarf, I thought I would send you a French postcard hoping you will get it safe. I think it a great pleasure to to have such a welcome article, especially from a little school girl. Well little friend, I wish you a Merry Christmas and the best of luck, again, hoping you will get this safe, I remain your friend.
A. Pusey, L/Cpl xxxxx
P. S. The words on Postcard means. Joyous Xmas. From a Woburn Soldier, Buckinghamshire.

Irene Ody, Womens Royal Flying Corp,
Port Meadow Airfield, 1917.
(Courtesy Michael Collins)

The 'Target' in reflective mood. Sole remaining
item of Port Meadow Airfield, 2010.

As a boy I would join the huge crowds that gathered around the War Memorial outside St Peters Church on Armistice day and listen to the names of those read out of who were killed in the Two Wars.

Among those gathered were several middle-aged ladies dressed in black. They would stand their with young children, tears streaming down their cheeks.

At the head of the procession behind the band my father as President of the British Legion would be leading all the old boys from Wolvercote trying their best to keep in step. All were immensely proud and wore their gleaming Great War medals with pride as if the Victoria Cross was one of them. They referred to them fondly as Pip, Squeak and Wilfred who were comic characters from their youth, a youth they spent within a rural upbringing, one that was about to be changed forever, the biggest change that had taken place since the division caused by the Canal and Railway some 140 years earlier.

The village life and rural atmosphere is hard to imagine today. Many had barely ventured beyond the county boundary. The call to serve King and Country in far off France was for many, too great a opportunity to miss in 1914. Husbands, fathers, brothers, sons and, to a lesser degree daughters, all enlisted in the armed forces, mainly the Army where the demand was greater. The Navy attracted fewer men due to the length of service they had to commit themselves to. At the outbreak of the War the Royal Flying Corp had yet to be formed.

Whenever Armistice Day came round when at school Bill Fallows recited a poem by Wilfred Owen and made sure we learnt it.

"Always remember, not just the poem, but the sacrifice they made for us", he said. It's entitled:

Anthem for Doomed Youth

What passing-bells for these who die as cattle?
Only the monstrous anger of the guns.
Only the stuttering rifles' rapid rattle
Can patter out their hasty orisons.
No mockeries now for them; no prayers or bells,
Nor any voice of mourning save the choirs,
The shrill, demented choirs of wailing shells;
And bugles calling for them from sad shires.

May they all rest in peace.

On the eleventh hour of the eleventh day of the eleventh month 1918 the armistice was signed. Peace such as it was, was very fragile and just two months short of 21 years Britain was again at war with what had become Nazi Germany - our old foe.

Extracts from Wartime Parish Magazines 1939-1945

Extracts from Wartime Parish Magazines as written by the Rev Paul Rebbeck, Vicar of St Peters Church. They paint a wonderful picture of the period at that time.

OCT 1939.
September opened with news that Poland has been invaded, we know that the general conflagration was inevitable, really inevitable, but for two days our minds were full of contending hopes and fears. We hoped that somehow we would still avoid the horrors of war. It was almost a relief to know on the 3rd September that the worst had come to the worst.

*   *   *

I have drawn up a 'WAR ROLL', a list of those serving His Majesties Forces, the names are those who were in the forces when the war started.

Norman Collett, Clifford Stone, Leslie Collett, Graham Clanfield and John George, all are in the Army. Maurice Simmonds, in the Navy.

NOV 1939.
I am happy that the rationing of petrol may make a difference in our Sunday School. We need more help than ever now that we have a large number of evacuee children. With cars standing idle in the garage instead of going off into the country, they will now be free to help the evacuee children. In this district, they are mostly from Poplar, they are very ready to be friendly. I have been greatly impressed by the kindness which has been shown to them in all parts of the parish.

JUNE 1940.
Writing in the Parish Magazine is never easy, because so much is happening so quickly, the whole situation may be changed by the time this letter reaches your homes. The war is making it very hard to keep up our supply of servers.

*   *   *

Mr & Mrs Griggs have received the sad news that their only son Roy, lost his life during a raid at a port in Western France.

As the B.E.F. had no resting place in France for it's feet at the beginning of June. I expect that copies of the Parish Magazine mis-carried. We are thankful to know that nearly all from this part of the world are safely back in England. Three of them are wounded, they are Tom Hands, Leslie Collett and George Weston, he being the most seriously wounded.

*   *   *

Oh Dear! Sad news. Walter Long, our Organist and Choir-master has received his calling up papers. Who will take on this onerous task?

Wartime Poster urging us to save food scraps (can't imagine that there were any!), 1940.

Left: The Rev Paul Rebbeck with his wife Dorothy and daughter Ann, 1935.
Right: Stan Revell and a herd of cows in 1944 waiting for morning service!

Evacuee children Ronnie and Brian Ford on right. With Tony, Bob and Cecily Pratley outside 11 Ulfgar Rd, 1939. (Courtesy Kathleen Pratley)

Les Collett aged 16 serving with 4th Battalion Oxford & Bucks Light Infantry.

Les Collett, after recovering from his wounds he was transferred to the Army Catering Corp, 1944.

Maurice Simmonds, Royal Navy, 1939. (Courtesy David Howard)

Letter from Field Service Hospital in France, informing his mother that Les has been wounded, 1940 (continued on the following two pages).

NOTHING is to be written on this side except the date and signature of the sender. Sentences not required may be erased. If anything else is added the post card will be destroyed.

[Postage must be prepaid on any letter or post card addressed to the sender of this card.]

I am quite well.

~~I have been admitted into hospital.~~

~~{ sick }~~ ~~and am going on well.~~

~~{ wounded }~~ ~~and hope to be discharged soon~~

~~I am being sent down to the base.~~

I have received your { ~~letter dated~~ _____
~~telegram~~ ,, _____
parcel ,, _____ }

Letter follows at first opportunity.

I have received no letter from you

{ lately
~~for a long time~~ }

Signature only } *L Callett*

Date _____

Forms/A2042/7.   51-4997.

Army regulation form from Les with B.E.F. in France to his mother in 1940.

Army Council form to Mrs Collett informing her that Les is wounded.

8th Battalion Oxford Home Guard (Wolvercote Division). Affiliated to Oxford & Bucks Light Infantry, taken in front of St Edward's School Boathouse, Godstow Road, 1940. Back row, left to right: ?, ?, Holiday, Lionel Halsey, ?, Alf Robinson, Alf Churchouse, Bert Allen, Jim Neal. 4th row: Ted Churchouse jnr, Noel Sutton, Hubert Humphries, Alec Stone, ?, Arthur Millard, Wilf Godwin. 3rd row: Ron Dawson, ?, Ralph Bowles, Frank Crozier, Stan Payne, ?, Nevin, Tom Green, Val Mapson, ?, Jim Pratley, Vic Surman. 2nd row: Ted Churchouse snr, ?, Capt Davies Potter, ? Davies, Alf Gomm. Front row: Cyril Towersey, John Fitzgerald, George Saunders, Ernie Loveridge, ? Allen, F. Mayo, George Bidmead, Gary Walker, Bob Dorrill. (Courtesy Bryan Sutton)

JAN 1941.

The illness and death of Dorothy C. Stockford during the Christmas festival, was a shock to many besides those of her home circle. Widespread sympathy is felt with Jack Stockford and his two young sons, John and Michael. Only a few days before her going from us, Mrs Stockford brought her two sons to church when John received communion.

*   *   *

Congratulations to Keith Stockford, promoted to Sergeant, and to Arthur Cox, Lance Cpl.

*   *   *

Will all readers of the magazine pay their 2/- for 1941, when the distributer calls.

APRIL 1941.

Mr H. O. King has been showing me a very vigorous poem, in which he denounces the painting of lips and finger-nails. I agree with him that the practice is a unpleasant one. It annoys me to see women coming to receive the Sacrament with lips smeared with lipstick, and hands that resemble bloodstained talons of birds of prey, but I don't think it worth while to spend time denouncing the practice. There are worse things that should arouse our indignation or our sorrow. Dishonesty, lax ideas about sexual morality, the raining down of murder and sudden death upon the homes of women and children. If it is a sin to paint, it is a comparatively trivial one.

MAY 1941.
There were excellent congregations on Good Friday and Easter Sunday. We have never had so many communicants. It is fortunate we now posses 3 chalices.

JUNE 1941.
So much has happened during the last twelve months, that Dunkirk evacuation seems to be in the remote past, but it is just a year since we heard how ships of all sorts and conditions were engaged in bringing the B.E.F. back to England. Just a year since we saw those hungry, exhausted, sun-scorched men marching down to Port Meadow. Ransacked our larders to give them tea and supper.

                          *   *   *

Mrs Hastings has received notification that her son Gilbert, is missing in action in the Middle East.
    Similar sympathy is felt for Mrs Simmonds, her son Maurice who was home on leave only a few weeks ago, has been reported missing, presumed drowned.

JULY 1941.
How difficult it is living in the same house as the Organist and Choir-master, as every meal time I am asked, "What Hymns are we having on Sunday?" I reply that I am very busy, what with gardening, visiting and having to write a sermon, I don't have time to think of such things. I then am confronted with "I simply must know, the boys are anxious to know what they are singing on Sunday." My suggestion that they could sing the same hymns as they sang three weeks ago didn't help, only to be told that just would not do. I replied that "If they came to church more often, they would know all the tunes." What a trial it is having one's dear wife as the Organist and Choir-master!

AUGUST 1941.
The evacuation officer wishes it to be known that more accommodation is needed for evacuated children.

SEPT 1941.
The diocese of Singapore is very much on the map, in these very anxious days there.

                          *   *   *

Councillor Bellamy is no longer Mayor, his two years Mayoralty are at a end.

Keith Stockford, Army Intelligence Corp, with mother and brother Lawrence outside 62 Godstow Road, 1940. (Courtesy Ann Stockford)

DEC 1941.

A letter has been received from Keith Stockford, he writes: I had rather hoped to be home at the end of 1941. Perhaps I can have the same hopes at the end of 1942. The ravages and horrors of this war which has brought so much destruction and death to England and other parts of the world.

DIEU VOUS GARDE.

JULY 1942.

Congratulations to the Sunday School! Yet another record. 5192, or £5-8s-2d. Of this total £1-2s-6d was contributed in silver (1080 farthings), 14/7½d in pennies and half-pennies, £3-11s-0½d in farthings (3410). It is said that the Treasurer had to make several journeys to the bank. The weight of 3000 farthings is staggering. A cheque for £5-8s-2d was presented to the Bishop at the Cathedral on the Thursday after Whit-Sunday by Michael Stockford and Bernard Tollett, who had the honour of representing the Sunday School. Over 70 children made use of envelopes, including some very small children in the junior classes who have begun to do their little bit for the Church at a early age. It is impossible to publish the full list. Those whose names are not among the names printed overleaf must not think that their gifts are despised, The record was reached because all worked together so keenly. Those who could collect 100 helped; and those who collected helped too.

Margaret	Chamberlain	426
Miss	Dubois	376
Mrs	Rebbeck	350
Michael	Stockford	204
Barbara	Pitson	153
Pauline	Brooks	151
Bernard	Tollett	140
Shelia	Moody	129
David	Sawer	129
Daphne	Long	126
Dorothy	Smith	118
Jean	Richardson	112
Roger	Davis	110
Brian	Stone	93
Beryl	Stone	93
Irene	Harris	84
Maude	Harms	70
Joyce	White	65
Miss	Waine	62
Sylvia & Rene	Keen	62
Ann	Truby	54
Betty, Mary & Kathleen	Smithson	54
Lily	Anderson	51
Miss	Strong	51

OCTOBER 1942.

As I came up Woodstock Rd on my faithful bicycle, my mind was mainly occupied with lighting-up time. I had come out to meet my Bishop, and was foolish enough to take no lamps with me. But in the intervals between my periods of anxiety the same uneasy thought insisted on coming back. The task before the Church is to relate Christianity to modern life, to the needs of the present day, still more to show the relation between Christianity and this busy, noisy world of buses and lorries and traffic-lights and coupons and rations and casualty-lists. It is no small task.

*   *   *

Mrs Alfred Loveridge (formerly Beulah Cox) has been informed that her husband is a Prisoner of War in Italy.

MAY 1943.

My dear People,

When I wrote my April letter I had not fully grasped that Mr Adcock would no longer be with us officially when the May Magazine was published. So I omitted to say a proper good-bye. But it is not too late to rectify the omission. I am sure you would wish me to say that good-bye, meaning by the words. May God be with you at Dorney and to thank Mr Adcock for all the help he has given us in the two years he has been here. In ordinary times we should have chartered a coach and made up a party to represent Wolvercote at his induction which will take place somewhere about the middle of May. But conditions being what they are, we must be content to wish him well from a distance in that fellowship of prayer with which even a great war cannot interfere. At present I have not heard of anyone to succeed Mr Adcock, and I may have to carry on single-handed for a bit. I hope you will not expect me to be in all parts of this sprawling parish at once. There are such things as physical impossibilities. And I hope you will not stop supporting the Assistant Curate Fund. Now is the chance to get a little ahead of our needs... if a successor to Mr Adcock cannot be found. That reminds me, I think we ought to ask our subscribers to pay up rather earlier in the year. In 1942 there were roughly 150 subscribers. More than 100 of them paid in the second half of the year, and 40 of the 100 in November and December.

*   *   *

You will accuse me of spending too much time over figures, and of filling this magazine with statistics. Well, if that is one of my sins, I am following a good example, I sin in company with another Vicar of Wolvercote, Bernard Attlee, who passed away in March. He must have spent a considerable amount of time on figures. The careful lists which he left behind show that the communicants at Easter 1901 numbered 116. At Easter 1909 they were 225. At Christmas 1901 there were 68 communicants. In 1908 there were 166. In 1905 he presented 47 candidates for Confirmation. (The late Mr. H. O. King often told me that in Mr Attlee's day they talked of enlarging the church).

*   *   *

But he was not really interested in figures. He was interested in people; and I know he was very fond of the people of Wolvercote parish. He was always pleased to be asked to preach in our church and always glad to hear news about his friends here, and Mrs Attlee gave me the sad privilege of taking the service at the crematorium on the day before the funeral at Holywell, because she knew her husband was so happy at Wolvercote, and she told me she wanted a Vicar of Wolvercote to conduct it.

*   *   *

Dr Attlee left Wolvercote more than 30 years ago. The population of the parish is now three times what it was in his day, and I am afraid that we cannot honestly say that there is any need to enlarge the church. But we shall have to do something after the war to provide better accommodation for the swollen Sunday School. And our Baptisms are becoming a problem too. We frequently have four baptisms on one Sunday. That means twelve godparents with minister and clerk in the small space round our font. Won't go.

APRIL 1944.
Good Friday Cinema Service. Will all readers please tell their friends that the Ritz Cinema has again been engaged and that there will be two Lantern Services, at 5-30 (by the Lord Bishop of the Diocese) and at 7-30 (by the Lord Bishop of Dorchester). Admission free. No children will be admitted unless accompanied by adults. Music by the Cinema Organ.

*   *   *

By the way, can anyone tell me what has happened to our woodpecker? The one which yaffled about the churchyard and the vicarage garden all the autumn?

Ritz Cinema, George Street, Oxford, 1944.

Upper Wolvercote youth, with Green Road in the background. Humphris shop is the first left-hand gable. From left to right they are: Brian Taylor, Ernest Saxton, John Stockford, ?, John Humphris, ?, Bert Saxton, Fred Saxton, 1943.

JUNE 1944.

The members of the Church Council seem to be of the opinion that it is high time I did some more money-raising. Personally I feel that I have spent a large part of my little life in appealing for money-first for the Church Roof, then the Organ, then for the Vestries and more recently for the Assistant Curate Fund — I deserve a rest.

*   *   *

Sympathy is offered to Mr and Mrs Bridgeman and to Mrs Sidney Bridgeman. It has now been "officially assumed" that Sidney who was missing after flying operations in Italy last autumn has lost his life. He was married in Wolvercote Church less than three years ago and his little son was baptised at our font last March.

SEPTEMBER 1944.

Aubrey Gurney's death in July has been followed by two more. Geoffrey Tipton died in a R.A.F. Hospital on 8th July, both were very useful members of our choir. John Cox of Ulfgar Road died on 6th August, he served in the Army.

*   *   *

So we are to have another Day of Prayer, I see. Yes it was given out on the wireless last night. Personally I am rather sorry. You mean we are getting into the sixth year of the war? Well we are all sorry about that. You'll have to put up those black-out shutters again, I'm afraid, instead of making a bonfire of them. But you didn't really expect the war to end as soon as we landed in France, did you? The news is splendid, of course, but we are still a long way from the Rhine, as General Eisenhower told us the other day. No, I mean I am sorry there is to be another Day of Prayer, I don't agree with them. That's a bit perverse on your part. Excuse me saying so vicar. Liver out of order? Try Curemall Chronic Capsules! I should have thought the clergy would be pleased to have a few more people in church. Besides every Sunday ought to be a National Day of Prayer. If the King picks out certain Sundays in this way, people think they need not bother about the other Sundays. They think they have done their duty if they come to church and patronise religion two or three times a year on these special days. No wonder Sunday is almost extinct.

NOVEMBER 1944.

THE VICARS WARDEN, as a consequence of the black-out no longer be required for churches, has been very busy removing the plywood discs from the circles at the top of the windows and patiently rubbing the black paint off those windows which could not be curtained or shuttered when the black-out was instituted.

THE PEOPLES WARDEN has been busy too. He has been shedding light....on the traffic problems of Oxford....illuminating the minds of the citizens by means of a book.

THE VICAR has been busy too, watching the vicar's warden cleaning windows, reading the people's warden's book & trying to discover it's inner meaning.

*   *   *

Has anyone tried to calculate how much boot-leather and how much tyre-rubber the clergy wear out unnecessarily when they have to visit a house at the end of Upland Park Road after visiting a house in Apsley Road? Or similarly, if they are calling to see a invalid at the far end of Rosamund Road and then looking up a Sunday School absentee at the end of Home Close? Has anyone ever reckoned how much longer it takes the people in Apsley Road and Upland Park Road to come to church because they have to travel via the Banbury Road and Davenant Road instead of coming straight into the Woodstock Road, as in a properly planned town.

MAY 1945.

The Third Army has entered Hanover.

The Canadians have by-passed Mannheim.

British heavy-bombers visited Breslau last night.

I have heard of these places before. I have seen them in my hymn-book.

Hanover is the name of the tune we use for "Disposer Supreme". In some churches it's used for "O worship the King".

Mannheim is 281, "Lead us heavenly Father", the hymn which seems appropriate for almost any occasion.

Breslau is the tune to "What various hindrances".

The Epiphany hymn "Earth has many a noble city" is sung to Stuttgart.

Number 34, the Sunday hymn which **we** often have at Choral Eucharist is sung to Lubeck. All these hymn-tunes — except Hanover which is English in spite of it's name — have a German origin. To extend the list, half our Easter hymns come from German sources. The Alleluia Processional we sing to Lasst Uns Erfreuen. "At the Lamb's High Feast" to Salzburg. "Christ the Lord is risen again" to Wurtenburg. The mention of Easter hymns turns my thoughts from tunes to words. Somehow the lines keep coming into my mind, "For Judah's Lion bursts His chains. Crushing the serpents head".

This is what we have to do. That is what we have we have almost succeeded in doing. Crush the serpent's head. But that task need not make us forget what we owe to Germany of former days. And the recollection will help us to hope for the coming of happier times. Cruelty, brutality, ruthlessness may be reigning supreme in the Germany of today, but there must be a Christian element left in German life.

There must be Germans who love to sing their Mannheim, their Stuttgart, their Lasst Uns Erfreuen. May their influence count for more in post-war Germany!

May common interests — and common beliefs — bind us together once more!

*   *   *

Congratulations to Tony Hewlett who staggered up with a bag containing 1,700 farthings.

JUNE 1945.

So Victory Day has come and gone. Our celebrations are over. The serpent's head has been crushed — in Europe. I read what I have written. I put my pen down, and ask whether it is all true. The war has become so much a part of ordinary existence that many of us find it hard to grasp the fact that hostilities really ceased. We still wonder whether the aeroplanes which pass over our heads have been bombing Hamburg or Kiel. We turn on the wireless and are surprised because there is no mention of the Oder or the Moselle.

Ray Venney with brother Ken, 1990. (Courtesy Mary Venney)

I don't think our congregations were very good either on 8 May or on Thanksgiving Sunday, but if our congregations were not very big, I am sure they were serious and sincere. I was impressed by the way everyone entered into the praying and the singing. And I was impressed too by the way in which the Victory Celebrations fitted in with the season of the Church Year. If we had been asked to choose a date for V E Day, we could have hardly have chosen better than 8 May. Indeed I found that V E Day helped me to understand Ascension Day better. Just as we still have to win the fruits of the Victory in Europe, to make our Victory effective by giving real freedom to the peoples of Europe and securing justice for them, so we have to make our Lord's Victory effective.

*   *   *

There was a great muster at the wedding of Raymond Venney and Mary Stagg on the 28th April. Sunday School, Dramatic Society and Choir were well represented, and there was a very happy atmosphere of prayer and good-will in the service. Indeed it was one of the happiest of weddings I remember. Raymond and Mary start their married life in the days when the buying of household goods is a difficult problem, but they are rich in the things that matter.

*   *   *

We were sorry to hear that Percy Tollett had been wounded in Germany. A few days more and he would have come through, However, he is safe in England, and doing well.

Entries from My Wartime Diaries

1939

3rd September   WAR DECLARED.
At 12 o'clock I walked to the Church to see the Evacuees arrive.

17th September   H.M.S. COURAGEOUS SUNK.
Mum crying, Uncle Chris her brother on board.

14th December   GRAF SPEE SUNK By H.M S. ACHILLES, AJAX and EXETER.
Fetched some logs from Traffords.

1940

9th April   DENMARK INVADED.
Sugar Payne helped me paint the yard tables.

10th May   CHURCHILL BECOMES PRIME MINISTER.
Bought a Sexton Blake from Gillets.

14th May   HOLLAND SURRENDERS. L.D.V. FORMED.
Went to the village Hall to see Will Hay in Convict 99.

27th May   B.E.F. EVACUATING DUNKIRK. Gardening at School today.

28th May   BELGIUM SURRENDERS. Went in the Signal Box.

10th June   MUSSOLINI TAKES ITALY INTO WAR ON HITLERS SIDE.
Got 2 badges from Dunkirk soldiers on the meadow.

22nd June   FRANCE SURRENDERS.
Had gas mask and Air Raid Shelter drill at School.

14th July   BATTLE OF ATLANTIC BEGINS.
Arthur Simmonds had his rope out on the crocodile.

8th August   BATTLE OF BRITAIN BEGINS. Played Marbles. Won 27.

14th November   COVENTRY BLITZED. Read a Biggles book.

24th December   MUM NOT VERY WELL. Dad sent for the Doctor.

25th December   MUM TAKEN AWAY IN A AMBULANCE.
She gave me everyones presents and asked me to distribute them.

27th December   MUM DIED AT 10 past 8 THIS MORNING. Biked to Yarnton to
tell Uncle Len and Aunt Chris.

Len and Harry Trafford, 1939.

Will Hay, our film favourite in *Convict 99*.

Wills Cigarette Card of the Graf Spee, 1939.

Troops patiently waiting to be
evacuated from the beach at
Dunkirk, 1940. (Courtesy Oxford
Mail & Times)

Some of the lucky one's waiting to
embark, 1940. (Courtesy Oxford
Mail & Times)

Other's not so lucky - now Prisoners of War, 1940. (Courtesy Oxford Mail & Times)

Troops leaving Dover, en-route to transit camps, 1940.

A Dunkirk 'special' passing through Wolvercote with troops throwing out letters for us to post, together with threepence for the stamp, 1940.

A Oxford Mail photo with a caption which read 'Back from the hell of Dunkirk, the troops at the transit camp on Port Meadow give the thumbs up sign', 10th June 1940.

1941

10th May	INCENDIARY BOMBS DROPPED ON LONDON. Siren went twice. 9 o'clock and 5 in the morning.
12th May	RUDOLPH HESS FLEW TO SCOTLAND. A girl from Summertown School gave me some prunes.
24th May	H.M.S. HOOD SUNK, ONLY THREE SURVIVORS. Dad got two tins of ice cream wafers.
27th May	BISMARK SUNK. Jumped off Trout bridge 20 times.
22nd June	GERMANS INVADE RUSSIA. Had a ride on a barge.
14th November	H. M. S. ARK ROYAL SUNK. Had School dinner in Village Hall.
7th December	JAPANESE ATTACK PEARL HARBOUR. AMERICA DECLARES WAR. Went to Church.
10th December	H. M. S. PRINCE OF WALES AND REPULSE SUNK. Uncle Chris on board, hope he's alright.

1942

15th February	SINGAPORE SURRENDERS TO THE JAPANESE. Cut frozen over. Saw Uncle Charles in Home Guard Parade.
23rd October	EL ALAMEIN. MONTGOMERY ADVANCES. Went to Parks Road Museum.

Municipal Restaurant, George Street, Oxford, 1943.

My 'Prunes' girl. We married 10 years later in 1951.

Charles Stockford with wife Edith, before going on Home Guard duty on Sunday evening, 1942. (Courtesy Ann Stockford)

H. M. S. Hood, Wills Cigarette Card, 1941.

Charles Stockford 4th from left, back row, with Grimbly Hughes Division Home Guard, 1942. (Courtesy Ann Stockford)

1942 (*continued*)

22nd November GERMANS IN STALINGRAD.
Had dinner in the Municipal Restaurant.

27th November FRENCH FLEET SUNK.
Went to pictures, saw San Demetrio London.

1943

31st August ALLIES INVADE ITALY.
Made a rabbit hutch, saw Ron Stone.

9th September LANDED IN SALERNO.
Watched Land Army girls haymaking at Wytham.

1944

22 nd January LANDED ON ANZIO BEACH.
Mr Parry not at school today.

10th February BOMBED MOUNT CASSINO.
Had two sticks of chewing gum from a Yank.

5th June ALLIES ENTER ROME.
Went in cab of Bourton Grange, No. 6871 (see page 165).

6th June ALLIES LAND IN FRANCE.
Had a new cricket bat.

A truly amazing photograph, this group of Wolvercote children were returning home after picking bluebells in Wytham Woods. At the Trout Inn there was the usual crowd of American G.I.s, one of which asked if he could take a photo of them, to which Judy O'Neill replied "Only if you send me a photo". He obviously kept his word. Back row, left to right: Robin O'Neill, Jimmy Gray, Judy O'Neill, Kathleen Pratley, Ann Miller, Audrey Waine. Front row: Dennis O'Neill, Cicely Pratley, Bob Pratley, Tony Pratley. (Courtesy Kathleen Pratley)

Chewing gum wrappers given to schoolboy Michael Stockford by U S servicemen based in the Oxford area during W WII.
The above is the caption which is shown under some of the 37 that I donated to the Imperial War Museum, London.

Land Army girls haymaking, 1943.

The 'Good old day's', haymaking with the aid of steam in 1931.

'Women's Land Army' poster, 1942.

A recreated display of a typical WWII small shop at the Imperial War Museum, London.

A typical post-war scene, half the time they had no idea what was going to be available when they eventually reached the counter. (Courtesy Imperial War Museum)

Wolvercote girls employed at the mill on a trip to Southsea in 1952. Starting at left in back row: Mary Smithson, Mrs Truby, Ann Truby, Gertie Hewlett, Win Phipps, Connie Mitchell, Beatie Savage, Pauline Lambert, Lille Robbins, Lille Parsons, Linda Prescott. Front Row: Kath Walton, Norah Dorrill, Verona Collett, Muriel Howard, Ann Miller, Margaret Dorrill, Kathleen Pratley, Barbara Fletcher, Phyllis Harding. Note: All of the above are their maiden names. (Courtesy Kathleen Pratley)

Since 1940 the majority of food was rationed. Fruit such as bananas, oranges and the like. Ice cream was a thing of the past. Tom on his Walls tricycle was awaited with eager anticipation—he often didn't appear. We were not completely without sweets and chocolate during those years, having 'survived' on 2 ounces per person per week for ages.

A amusing story I remember about our first banana for years was when two children were taken on a train by their mother. As a surprise and a special treat she also bought them their first banana, a fruit they had never seen let alone eaten. The girl started to eat hers first at the very moment the train entered a long tunnel. She then anxiously asked her brother if he had eaten his yet. "No" he replied. "Then don't" she said "They make you go blind".

One day without warning or prior announcement a Ford van pulled up outside the church 'Ices of Quality. Carlo & Sons' was freshly painted on the sides and rear doors. Kids appeared as if by magic, unable to believe what they saw.

Unbelievably trade wasn't brisk: no-one had any money!

First ice cream for years. Carlos van waits for school trade 1946. Money must have been tight. Just one proud customer displays his purchase. Carlo's driver doesn't look that happy. There is an interesting error with this photo, can you spot it? (Courtesy June Gray)

Plenty of prospective customers with not a penny between them, 1946. (Courtesy June Gray)

Slowly but surely we adapted to our new found freedom, unlike the cuckoo heralding the arrival of Spring, the banana and ice cream did not herald the end of rationing. This would continue until the early 1950s, far longer than anyone expected.

Wages were some 20% higher than they were in 1939. Although overall people were better off, with continuing shortages life was very onerous. It took quite a few years to adapt to our hard fought freedom, eventually we took it for granted.

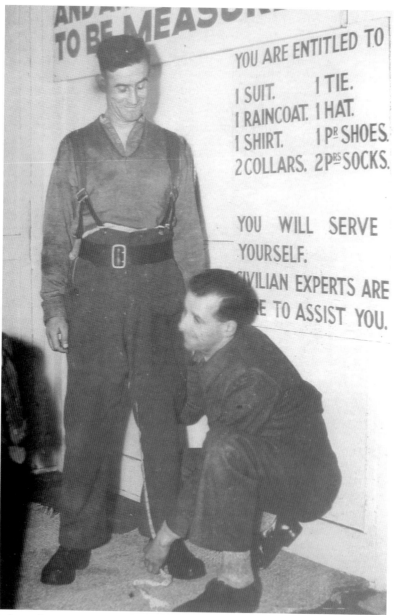

At least they were measured for their demob suit (unlike their uniform), 1946.

With Queen Mary on his right, Queen Elizabeth and King George VI take the salute at the Victory Parade in London, the largest of its kind ever seen, June 8th, 1946.

"The French will never forgive themselves for having lost the war. They'll never forgive the British for *not* having lost the war. But above all they will never forgive the Americans for having won it."

Winston Churchill, 1946

The Arrival of the 'Otters'

Other things we took for granted which we thought would go on forever, had also changed. Having served the Parish with dedicated pastoral care for a period of 22 years (longer than any of his predecessors) Paul Rebbeck, his wife Dorothy and three daughters who had lived all their lives in Wolvercote, had gone. For those of us who were teenagers when they left, had grown up with the Rebbecks, without them life seemed very strange and different. Whoever was appointed had a hard act to follow.

Full of apprehension all round, our new incumbent Michael Ottaway arrived, he was a bachelor. "We will show him what we want" the old die-hards said in unison, it didn't take him long with his gentle (but persuasive) manner to turn the tables on his sceptics.

Within a very short time, he, and his mother who could charm the birds off the trees, had the whole parish behind him, after which he slowly but surely began to put his own stamp on things.

In 1950 he organised a successful Christmas Pageant in St Peters. Two years later in 1952 he formed a Coronation Committee to welcome the new Monarch to the throne. He played a huge part in ensuring Wolvercote celebrated in style. It was in 1953 he changed the long familiar frontispiece of the Parish Magazine to one designed by Lawrence Dale, who he portrayed in a sketch of himself sitting at an easel in one corner, with a horned devil slinking off in the other. Pixey's playing on the mead, also number 2 and 4 buses represent the location in the parish.

 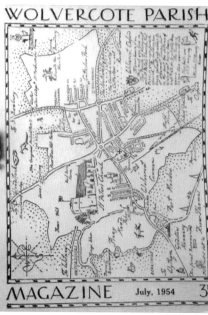

Wolvercote Parish Magazine, 1944 and 1954.

Charles Stockford (centre, wearing trilby) leaves the Town Hall after joining the huge crowd who were there to hear the announcement of the Accession to the Throne of Queen Elizabeth II, 1952.

Churchwarden A. Norrington, Vicar M. J. Ottaway and Verger K. White holds the tree. Churchwarden W. Godwin and N. Chamberlain look on approvingly, whilst the Mayor of Oxford, W. King, completes the tree planting ceremony to celebrate the Queens Coronation, 1953.

St Peters Church, floodlit for the Missionary Festival, 1956.

Nineteen-fifty-six was a eventful year for the whole Parish, who were delighted to share in the celebrations when Michael Ottaway's bachelorhood came to a end on 14th January with his marriage to Glenys Palmer by the Bishop of Oxford.

With the passage of time he had changed from being a bachelor, to a married man (following the birth of their daughter Helen) into a family man. Everyone was so pleased for both Michael and Glenys. Their joy turned to great sadness, following the birth of a second daughter Ann, who tragically died in infancy. They were totally devastated, as we all were. Sorrow turned to joy with the arrival of daughter Francis in 1960, to complete the family.

With his new family around him, Michael found new vigour and enthusiasm when he organised a team of volunteers headed by Wilf Godwin to build a much needed extension to the Church room, to provide a kitchen and toilets. It was suggested at the time, that providing he would open the toilets by being the first to use them at the opening ceremony, they would do it! The building was completed, without insisting he carried out the opening act. It was all done in good humour.

Later in the same year, he organised a fortnights mission, which began with a torchlight procession round the parish, its object was to help those who wanted to learn more about the faith.

For some considerable time in 1957, the tower bells were conspicuous by their absence, due to all six bells being recast to give a better tone. They were rededicated in July. After his first decade at St Peters he had done well, more changes had taken place in his life than he could have possibly imagined, he was affectionally known as 'Otters'.

The Stockford family in 1961, Jane, Michael and Richard.

Jane Stockford, choirgirl at St Peter's, aged 13, 1968.

Our pride and joy, 1961.

Rita and myself, together with our three children, Jane, Michael and Richard moved back to live in the Parish, following the purchase of 3 Carey Close. We all became actively involved with St Peters. I took on the duties of a Sidesman, Rita the Chairman of the Church Council. Jane who was friends of Helen Ottaway, joined her in the Choir, both Michael and Richard eventually became Servers.

Early in 1965, Michael Ottaway's sermon at the 9-30 service was entitled 'REDEEM THE TIME'. The text he explained was taken from the inscription that once enhanced the sundial on the tower, "How wonderful" he said "if only our sundial could be restored, but how and by whom?" "To prove that I listen to your sermon I will do it" I told him. On the way home Rita said "I didn't know you knew anything about sundials". "I don't but I'll have to find out won't I?" I visited The Central Library and took out all the books they had on the subject. As a result of information gleaned, it is almost certain that the original sundial dates back to the 15th century, this I discovered in going through the Church records, about to be deposited in the Bodlean Library. It was dated 1916 the entry was written by the Rev Edward A. Sydenham, who said that after Sunday lunch, Churchwarden Harry Chamberlain returned to the Church and between them they stripped the ivy that completely covered the tower and in so doing, pulled away the then inscription "Redeem The Time" which was in a poor state of repair.

Why two Gnomons? What were they for? How did they work and what was the lower single one on the southeast corner for? The only way to find out was a 15 hour watch on a sunny day; this came early in May. So it was that I arrived at Church at 5 a.m. The result - no shadow from either Gnomon. At 6 a.m. I was rewarded, my first shadow appeared. It was at the top left hand of the Gnomon on the south elevation; throughout the day it worked its way down and across to the right, disappeared on the east elevation at 4 p.m. at the bottom of the gnomon and worked its way up until 8 pm. when it disappeared altogether. The sundial is 'set' at Greenwich Mean time, not British Summer time, hence it's one hour 'slow' during this period. The lower Gnomen is the Matins sundial, the shadow cast from this strikes the angle of the stone on which it is fixed at that hour, 11 o'clock.

Having acquired the necessary information and knowledge I then made a mould and cast the letters and figures, all 45 of them.

For sundials to be correct it is preferable to set them on Midsummer's day the 26th June. In 1965 this fell on a Saturday which was most convenient as it was my day off work. My prayers were answered as it was a clear blue sunny sky all day. I arrived at Church at 4 a.m., hoisted my triple extension ladder, then each hour, on the hour marked the shadow cast from the Gnomen on the stonework. With barely enough time to fix the figure before the next hour arrived, time was of the essence.

Two enforced breaks were thrust upon me to allow two weddings to take place, with strict instructions from the Vicar that no sign of work taking place should be in evidence during the service, Rita had a equally arduous day, with three young children to look after, she walked to and from Church goodness knows how many times with food and drink to sustain me on what proved to be a extremely hot day.

At 9 p.m it was done - all finished. Michael Ottaway was keen to have it ready for the St Peters patronal festival the next day - I do remember, I slept well that night!

In the process of restoring 'Redeem the Time', 10.30 a.m., 26th June 1965.

All finished, 7.30 p.m.

Five faithful servants of St Peter's 1983. Left to right: Ken White, Bill Crumly, Ray Venney, John Beale and Norman Chamberlain.

In 1971 Michael Ottaway appointed me his Peoples Warden, with Bill Genese as the Vicars Warden (Bill was a really interesting chap, who had served as the Assistant Commissioner to Baden Powell the Chief Scout). It was during this period that the English Currency changed to the decimal system. Following a Sunday Service George Prince and myself who had been acting as Sidesmen, were in the process of counting the collection money, when in walked Bill who picked up a new twopence piece and closely examined it, then berated us for putting 'Foreign' currency in the banks bag. George was absolutely furious. I tried without success to calm things down. George resigned and walked out. Nothing I said could convince Bill that it was a coin of the realm, and that he was totally out of order, suggesting he owed George a apology. The following day I received a letter from Bill saying that he would resign at the Church Council meeting on Tuesday.

On Tuesday at a fully attended meeting Bill stood up and apologised. I jumped up, spoke for George and myself saying a mountain was being made out of a molehill. An explosive situation was defused - all over twopence!

I soon discovered that being Churchwarden was a very arduous task. I did not for a single moment imagine that it would entail being involved in subterfuge. The year 1974 marked the 25th anniversary of Michael Ottaway's induction as the incumbent of the parish of St Peters Wolvercote. It fell on 29th July. The date chosen to celebrate it was the Parish Fete, to be held on the 6th July. Those involved together with myself, were Martien Parmentier the Curate, Bill Genese, Peter Bridges and Evelyn Bryant.

Notices of the celebration were sent out with STRICTLY CONFIDENTIAL heading all correspondence, everyone passed on information in such a way it became almost comical, not to say amusing. It was great fun, and the secret never got out, the outcome was a huge success, as the report of the day written by Michael Ottaway confirms.

Your very generous act on the afternoon of 6th July, for which Glenys and I thank you with all our hearts, came as a complete surprise. More people had gathered in the garden than in previous years; the sunny weather must have brought them out, I thought. The Stockford family were standing in a group expectantly, Peter was loitering near by, Martien was no where to be seen and, when Bill at the microphone announced an important visitor, I was still unsuspecting. The bells began ringing; my watch said 2.30 —they must be getting ready for the 3.30 wedding! A figure in purple cassock flanked by two others with staves at the ready, appeared moving through the churchyard.

Glenys and I were collected and hurriedly shepherded forward to where the Bishop of Dorchester was standing, and there followed the most delightful ceremony. The Bishop made a gracious speech and, on behalf of you all, presented us with a picture of the ruins of Godstow Nunnery from a drawing 1784, and a document beautifully illuminated (you know by whom!) conveying your congratulations on my 25 years as

Twenty-fifth anniversary of Rev M. J. Ottaway's induction as priest, 29th June 1974. Christopher Swain leads the Choir, Rev Michael Ottaway and his wife Glenys on the right. (Courtesy Oxford Mail & Times)

Rev Michael Ottaway, daughter Helen, Jane Stockford and Christopher Swain, organist, 1974.

vicar and your love to us both and your gift of £350. Glenys received a lovely basket of flowers from Jessica Balls and Rachel Lane.

The Celebration Hymn— words by Roger Green and music by Christopher Swain—which was then sung by the choir delighted us by its humour and unpretentiousness, as well as giving us both a moment to compose ourselves before briefly and haltingly expressing our thanks. We shall often look back on that sunny afternoon at the parish fete as one of the happiest days of our lives. We have enjoyed every moment of our time here, and we felt that you were saying something very real about the pleasure it gave you too. I hope we shall be given a few more years in Wolvercote.

Glenys joins me in sending you our love and good wishes.

Festivals of Vicars

OTTAWAYS CELEBRATION HYMN

HYMN 25. St Peter's Chains - Irregular   Christopher Swain (1974)

All we who worship at St Peters
  as well as friends from far and near,
Rejoice with Michael and with Glenys
  upon this five and twentieth year.
For reaching this historic landmark
  we offer them congratulation.
We thank them for their years of service,
  their ceaseless toil and dedication.

For them "by voluntary subscription"
  Saint Peter's pence have been collected
To form a gift for our dear couple -
  we trust it will not be rejected,
Since money makes a boring present,
  we ask this blessed pair to choose
Whate'er they like to spend the cash on,
  from bedroom suite to sunshine cruise.

So thank you Michael, thank you Glenys,
    for all your selfless ministration;
And at this time let us remember
    we are a Christian congregation
So let us render last and first
    to God our gratitude and praise
For his great wisdom and discernment
    in sending us the Ottaways!

                                 Roger Green.

During my time as Churchwarden St Peters provided a coach which picked up those parishioners who lived in the Templar Road area, also Upper or Lower Wolvercote, who wished to attend Sunday morning Church services and found the long walk involved too much for them. This was very much Bill's idea. Over the years he fought tooth and nail to maintain this service; hours were spent at vestry meetings discussing it, always the same thing. "We can't afford it." "In that case I will pay for it out of my own pocket" would be Bill's stock answer, to be followed by "Don't talk rubbish Bill." He won every time - the coach continued to run, passengers having dwindled to no more than a dozen. As far back as I can remember, far more people from the lower part of the Village attended Church services than those from the upper part, the ratio remained the same after the increase in population after the 1930s.

The thing I remember most in what turned out to be Bill's last Christmas, was the Candelabrum, It's the one to the left of the porch door. It was Christmas midnight mass, the Church as usual was full to capacity, both Bill and myself were doing sidesman duties. He approached me and said "Don't you think you should do something about that Candelabrum, its bent." "Good lord Bill, that's been like that since time immemorial, why choose now to do it." I replied. "Are you going to do it, yes or no?" "No." "In that case I will do it myself ." With that he grabbed hold of the bracket (made of cast iron) and attempted to straighten it, the result being, it came away in his hand. "Help me" he wailed. "You pulled it off, you put it back" I unchristianly told him. He stood there holding it, the candles still burning. After some five minutes, which must have seemed like half an hour to him, I went to his rescue. "Help me Michael, I promise you I will never make any demands on you ever again." "Remember your in Church" I reminded him. "I promise", he replied. With that I relieved his aching arms and made it as secure as I was able under the circumstances.

"That will teach you to behave yourself" I said to him. "Till the next time" he said with a grin. "You forget that I have a direct line to the Almighty, he will forgive me."

Bill always said his wish would be, when his end came, he would hope to die in Holy Week. He must have had direct contact with the Almighty, as on Tuesday of that very week in 1975 he died, leaving me as the sole Warden to attend to no less than 16 services over the Easter period. Following Bill's death Desmond Walshaw was appointed as his successor.

It was at this time that a sum of money was bequeathed to the Church by a former Mayor of Oxford, Alderman Bellamy, to be used as a suitable memorial in memory of his late wife. What form would the memorial take? Many suggestions were

Michael Ottaway welcomes Bill Crumly and his flock. Following the arrival of the Sunday morning coach in 1972.

Michael Ottaway with draft sketch of Piper window, 1975.

put forward, although constructive, none provided that extra 'oomph' that was required. That was until Glenys Ottaway calmly said "Why don't we ask John Piper to design us a window?" Everyone just stared at her agape and asked "Are you being serious Glenys?" assuring us she most certainly was. Michael Ottaway turned to Desmond and told him to get on with it. I can only admire Desmond's effort, within a matter of days he reported back to say he had arranged a date for us to visit John Piper at his studio near Henley-on-Thames. Up to then I had to admit that my only knowledge regards John Piper was that he had designed the window in Coventry Cathedral.

One late spring evening I joined Desmond in Michael's Morris Minor Traveller, and the three of us headed towards Henley. Arriving at John Piper's house, he welcomed us and took us on a tour of his studio which was situated in a converted barn. Paintings were everywhere. I then realised what a wonderful experience and privilege it was for us. John Piper proceeded to put his ideas to us, among them one that signified the multitude cheering Christ's triumphant ride into Jerusalem on Palm Sunday which fired our enthusiasm. Our journey home was one of excitement and gratitude — we couldn't wait to see the draft sketches promised within a month.

If everything went according to plan, and we were in a position to approve one of the draft designs, the finished window could be dedicated at the Patronal Festival on June 29th. The service was planned to open the week-long Wolvercote Festival, so all the more reason to hope that things went well. In the weeks that followed the draft sketches were produced, the final one approved, John Piper set to work. With time running out, we received a call to say the window which was being made by a Canadian named Patrick Reyntiens would be delivered on the Friday. The previous evening I prepared the scaffold.

Nicolas and Anthony Green on the left appear to be having a telling off, Ann Cameron is making her way to the church room. Michael Ottaway is talking to what must be a very small person against the wall, as for me I don't look too pleasesd with the estimate I have received for a haircut! After the morning service, 1976.

I stand precariously balancing myself on
two pews having been told to do so by the
Bishop of Dorchester on the extreme left, he
is beside John Piper, while the Rev Michael
Ottaway presses his hand against my knee
to keep me steady, Patronal Festival, 1976.

St Peter's Church: Bellamy Memorial Window designed by John Piper, 1976.

Vicar and Choir at the dedication of the Loft-Simpson Memorial Garden, St Peter's Church, 1981.
Back row, left to right: Catherine Lack, Glenys Ottaway, Kelly Johnson, Eileen Wright, Evelyn Bryant,
M. J. Ottaway, ?, Viv Bridges, Ray Venney, Patrica Culme-Seymour, Bill Johnson, Jay ?. Among the
children are Daniel and Oliver Johnson and Isabel Nicholls. (Courtesy Eileen Wright)

At 10 o'clock the following morning Patrick Reyntiens arrived. "I can't stop, I've got a plane to catch" he said, and was gone. With it being a normal working day for me I returned to work, leaving the next day — Saturday — the only day left to install the window before the dedication ceremony on Sunday, I said a silent prayer!

During the evening I returned, unpacked the various panels, offered them up in position and nearly died - they were all too small; They had been made to the sight line with no allowance made for the extra width required for building in.

Only one thing for it, extend them all round with a strip of lead soldered on. It took me until late evening, it was dark when I finished.

With perfect weather, the eagerly awaited day arrived, the Church was packed to capacity with even standing room at a premium. Among the crowded congregation was the Lord Mayor of Oxford, Councillor Anne Spokes, not only a parishioner, but a regular member of the congregation. John Piper was also present. The Bishop in his sermon said "A window like this is a priceless gift from day to day, because of its freshness and delight". It truly was a memorable occasion. John Piper asked me if I was pleased with the result. I felt very humble!

Over the subsequent years it has drawn a huge amount of interest. As a memorial to the late Alderman C. J. V. Bellamy and his wife Maud, they couldn't have imagined in their wildest dreams that such a wonderful window would have been dedicated to them.

In 1980 after serving as Peoples Warden for 10 years. I told Michael Ottaway that it was not my intention to surpass that period of 23 years set by Wilf Godwin, and the time had come for me to stand down. It was then that he told me, that he himself would be retiring in 1983, and he would like me to carry on and see the new incumbent settled in. I felt totally devastated, the thought of him retiring had never entered my train of thought and just couldn't imagine St Peters without him and Glenys.

After lots of thought and soul searching I retired as Peoples Warden in 1981, leaving enough time for my successor, Peter Bridges to work alongside Desmond Walshaw to assist Michael's replacement, 'as and when' he arrived.

So it was, after 53 years the two Vicars of the parish who had played such a huge part in, not only mine, but in Michael's case, Rita's and our childrens life - had gone. On 19th December 1992 Michael John Ottaway celebrated the Jubilee of his Ordination to the Priesthood, although he and Glenys now lived in Sussex, his wish was that the celebration take place at Wolvercote, where for so long he was our much loved Parish Priest for 37 years.

A Celebration Mass was held in St Peter's at 12 noon on Saturday 19th December 1992 followed by a buffet lunch in the Village Hall attended by 119.

Following the Service and Lunch, both of which were not only happy, but emotional occasions, Michael commented that both he and Glenys were grateful for making the whole day (as indeed our time at St Peters was) such a wonderful nostalgic occasion. This not only echoed mine, but also all of us who were privileged enough, to share those years with him.

The Village Baptist Church

Residents of Wolvercote who were Church of England, were well served by St Peters Church. Those of other faith's, would have to travel to Oxford to worship. Summertown had the Congregational Church, those stalwarts of the Baptist faith had the long trek to New Rd. A prominent local Baptist was Ernest Alden, a member of the respected family who supplied meat from their shops in the town centre.

Ernest Alden would preach at the Whit Monday Fair held on the green in front of the Red Lion during the latter part of the 19th Century. Ignoring the amount of ale that had been consumed, he took advantage of the crowd who had processed through the village behind the band and the members of the Ancient Order of Foresters, who retired to their clubroom. With a Fairground held on the Green, it must have been a challenge to make himself heard, none-the-less he did, and although well 'tanked up', they lent him a sympathetic ear. In a effort to provide a place to worship Mr Fred Norrish offered the use of his Cottage as a venue, (later demolished for road widening). This was subsequently followed by the use of a Barn belonging to Alderman George Cooper who was a baker, Harry Collett built a platform and provided seats, this was used until 1886. By this time things had really begun to progress in a very positive way. Ernest Alden's perseverance and enthusiasm came to fruition. On Whit Monday (when else!) the 14th June 1886, the foundation stone of the present Baptist Church was laid. Ernest Alden proclaimed that the tender submitted by Mr Hutchins for £ 345 had been accepted to build a Chapel that would seat 150 people, there would also be a ancillary room adjacent to the main building, this would contain a copper and provision to store coal, also included would be a suitable room to be used as a Vestry.This would increase the overall cost to £400. With promises made, (work had already started) more was urgently needed, A Band of Hope, a Sunday School and a Clothing Club would make use of the new facilities, they were asked to help raise the necessary cash.

Although a wet day over 200 people attended the stone laying ceremony. A total of 6 stones were laid. Under the stone laid by the Mayor of Oxford, Alderman Robert Buckell (who was a member of the New Road Church) was placed a bottle containing a copy of the Oxford Chronicle. New Road Mission plans, and a copy of Ernest Alden's statement. Following the stone laying ceremony, they made their way to George Coopers barn where tea was provided, more speeches followed before the dedication service.

Wolvercote Baptist Church Sunday School, 1886. (Courtesy Gerald Collett)

Gerald Collett at Baptist Church entrance, 2011.

Various pledges were made, one parishioner pledged to give up smoking for a year, the 26 shillings saved, would be given to the fund. A grand total of £160 was pledged, a truly remarkable achievement. Even more, was the fact that on the 15th Sept 1886 a mere 3 months after work started, the Chapel was finished. The only conclusion that can be drawn from this is that Mr Hutchings could not have had any other work on, or, he had a amazing number of tradesmen working for him. Even the cost was within the estimate of £400. The seats from the old barn were used until 1889, when new pews which had been made by Dan and Alf Collett were installed.

In his 32 years he served as minister until his retirement in 1916, the Rev James Dunn received 565 members into the faith, and baptised no less than 691.

Two years after the Chapel was completed, a further extension was added to provide a Schoolroom Hall, at a further cost of £170. This emphasized the huge following the Baptist Church had at that time. At the commencement of the Great War in 1914, the amazing number of children attending Sunday School was 130 with 11 teachers.

The Baptist Church like St Peters, enjoyed it's largest congregation at this time, after the Great War the number of church goers went into decline.

With the passage of time, it's inevitable that things change, the Baptist Church was no exception. It was then that Dan Collett became actively involved with the church. The strong support for the Baptist Church shown by Dan has continued unbroken for a century through his family, with grandson Gerald continuing the strong Collett tradition, I, and many others of my generation entered the Baptist Church for the first time in 1939 when, as a result of the school being unable to cope with extra children in the form of evacuees from London, it was used as a class-room. It took 3 years before normality returned.

May the love and determination that created the Baptist Church, continue for another 100 years.

The National Association of Boy's Clubs - Woppin' Branch

As youngsters I can't say that we were guilty of getting into much mischief, with P.C. Pike (or Pikey as we called him) doing irregular rounds on his bike. It was more than our lives were worth to have him march us home by our ear, he always gave us the choice of, as he put it. "Shall I deal with it, or shall we go and see your Father." It was no contest! "You deal with it Constable Pike" (we knew when we were well off!). There was not a lot we could get involved in due to lack of adult supervision. The men (and women) who would have supervised us, were away on active service. Cubs and Scouts were 'put on hold' with no one to run them, we used to meet in the now deserted Du Merrick's farm at the back of Cyprus Terrace. To provide an alternative, a group of enthusiastic men led by Mr Norrington and Father Carter from the Roman Catholic Church, SS Gregory & Augustine on the Woodstock Rd, put their enthusiasm into forming a Boys Club into practice, they recruited the help of masters and teachers

Wolvercote Boys Club members, 1946. Left to right: Digger Holder, Fanny Souch, ?, Skuzzy Stone with dog, Ken Quartermain, Gobber Gascoyne, Sugar Payne, Brian Taylor, Aubrey Dorrill, Geoff Long and Skip Martin. (Courtesy Oxford Mail & Times)

from St Edwards School, as a result, by inviting the then Warden The Rev Henry Kendall to become a patron of the club, and join them on the Committee. This was a very shrewd move indeed, they were already supporting a Boys Club in Bermondsy, distance prevented members from that area gaining the practical use of not only the many sporting activities but also providing coaches for the various types of sport that St Edwards were able to offer, this included the Boat House at Godstow along with tuition in rowing.

All of this was taking place during a crucial time during May 1940. With the British Expeditionary Force in full retreat in France huge activity was taking place in England to accommodate the inevitable, that being the mass evacuation of our forces from France, Pill Boxes were being built in the most unusual places along the canal and in obscure places across 'meadow and lea'. On the practical side a Local Volunteer Defence (later the Home Guard) was formed. St Edwards School, always eager and ready to help others, became attached to the 6th Battalion Oxford Division itself affiliated to the Oxford & Bucks Light Infantry. Port Meadow was considered a vulnerable area for German parachutists to land, St Edwards having close to one hundred boys who enrolled in the L.D.V. plus the added bonus of being armed with rifles from the school's combined cadet force armoury, compared to the majority having to make do with pitchforks and the like, were given the plum job of providing a 24 hour watch on Port Meadow under the eye of J. M. Gauntlett, a master from the science department, small in stature and immense in heart and popularity.

Towards the end of May a large number of workmen descended on the meadow and drove a series of four inch diameter wooden stakes at an acute angle at strategic areas around the meadow, now out of bounds to all, it transpired that the stakes were there to prevent parachutists landing! A patrol from the school provided the necessary guard and patrolled nightly at the boat house keeping a alert look out for the expected parachutists, one morning they were more than a little surprised to discover that overnight a forest of Army Bell Tents had sprung up in the darkness ready for the arrival of the Expeditionary Force, to which the guards replied "I thought I heard something in the night". To the dismay of the boys and the relief of the authorities and the army, they were transferred to less demanding duties. That being road-block duties on the Witney by-pass where they couldn't do any harm — could they?

Armed with nothing more than extreme enthusiasm and coils of barbed wire they took up their positions and waited for disguised enemy paratroops to appear. When what they considered to be a suspicious looking lorry approached they proceeded to stretch the barbed wire across the by-pass bringing the traffic to a screeching halt, on inspection the back of the lorry contained a bunch of R.A.F. personnel en route for a night out in Oxford. Anyone who has had anything to do with barbed wire is more than aware that it's very easy to stretch it out, but quite the opposite to roll it back up, which in this instance proved the case, It took hours to clear the back-log of military traffic that had accumulated. It was decided that despite their eagerness to help the war effort, it was a lot more practical - and safer to confine them to the school grounds. Fortunately this enthusiasm from the various coaches and facilities that the school offered the Boys Club was put to great advantage and hugely appreciated throughout the war.

With such a eager team behind it, the club was destined to go from strength to strength, the only obstacle being, you had to be 10 years old before you were allowed to become a member. When the great day arrived I well remember walking up the lane from The Plough with nervous apprehension, on arriving at the door I opened it, pulled the blackout curtain to one side to be greeted by Mrs Crozier, her daughter Kathy, Mrs Waine and Connie. "Come on in my duck and have a cup of tea" they said offering me a cup together with a bath-bun. With a welcome like that, I was soon at my ease, when you are at the tender age of ten, those who are but one or two years older, adopt a superior air, you are in awe of them to say the least. The first to appear was Brian Rivers and Pete Walker, "Come on young Stocky, let us show you around and see what you are interested in." I followed them around a absolute labyrinth of passages, hoping I wouldn't lose sight of them, for fear that I would never find my way out.

Frank Crozier, a boys club stalwart.

Wolvercote Boys Club Canteen Ladies, 1946. Kathy Crozier, Nora Martin, Gladys Crozier, Mrs Stanfield. (Courtesy Kathy Rivers)

Excluding outdoor sports and games, there was Boxing; Darts; Dominoes; Billiards and Snooker; Table Tennis; Drama classes and a well stocked Library in a Quiet room (that's the last thing it was). To summarize, there was something to satisfy everyone's taste, the only thing that I was not keen on, was boxing, and that I learned was as good as compulsory. It will toughen you up I was told, to which I replied that I was tough enough. I still had to partake, one evening Reg Buckle and myself were chosen to go for three rounds. Reg pushed me away, I stumbled back against the angle of the fireplace recess, which caught me between my shoulder blades and suffered a nasty bruise. I 'played' on it, my boxing days were over!

Although the War was over National Service continued, this meant that when you reached the age of 18, you were called up to do eighteen months service (increased to 2 years in 1948) the only chance you had to avoid it, was if you were serving an apprenticeship as I was. In which case you were deferred until the apprenticeship was completed, you gained two more years, but the inevitable still happened, you had to go.

This naturally made a big difference to all of us, choice never entered the equation. This ultimately played havoc with those involved in Football and Cricket. With players forever being called up, it was difficult to maintain a good side, which meant those who were not the best, at least had a chance to prove themselves.

Wolvercote Boys Club Football XI, 1946. Back row, left to right: Les Waine, ?, Peter Parker, Brian Rivers, Roy Parsons, Tom Dicks, Ray Butler, Bill Hiett, Pete Walker. Front row: Geoff Hibbins, Dave Walker, John Cox, Bert Green, Reg Buckle.

Wolvercote Football Team outside The Red Lion, 1946. Back row, left to right: Geoff Long, Ron Welsted, Roy Parsons, James Pratley, Jim Waine, Bob Dorrill. Front row: John Fitzgerald, Colin Ford, Frank Williams, John Cox, Arthur Warmington.

Wolvercote Boys Club Committee Members, 1946. Back row, left to right: Frank Spiers, Geoff Hibbins, Reg Buckle, John Cox, Perce Hambridge. Front row: Les Waine, John Allen, Pete Walker, Brian Rivers.

Wolvercote Boys Club Table Tennis Team, 1948. Left to right: Tony Taylor, Vic Gascoyne, John Saxton, John Payne, Ken Quarterman.

With the end of hostilities, a recently demobbed chap by the name of Harry Martin was appointed leader of the club, releasing voluntary helpers who had coped so well over the years. Les Waine, Mr Crozier and others had done a splendid job, together with Pete Walker, John Allen, Geoff Hibbins, John Cox, Jimmy Gray, Tom Dix and Brian Rivers (who like myself was a Landlord's son. His father kept the Red Lion in Lower Wolvercote). "We should be grateful to them all," said Skip Martin. "Not forgetting all the ladies, together you have provided a stable platform to continue the good work they have so selfishly done for so long. Your continued help will be greatly appreciated."

Harry (Skip) and Norah Martin, 1946.

Alice and Gilbert Rivers, landlord and landlady of the Red Lion. (Courtesy Kathy Rivers)

With a new leader everyone got stuck into brightening the old place up. It was painted top to bottom. If I found it difficult to find my way around the club prior to it being redecorated, at least then each room was a different colour, which helped, now it was green and white everywhere, it was totally confusing. Skips explanation was, that in our search for a certain room, we would discover activities taking place that we were totally unaware of. Our explanation was, that he bought a load of paint cheap off the back of a lorry! Surprisingly enough, his theory worked, we all discovered new interests. This wasn't the only idea of Skips that gave us the opportunity to become involved. He came up with the idea of a Quarterly Magazine, the whole thing to be written, edited and printed by Club members, this ambitious, exciting project put fire in our bellies, we entered into it with great enthusiasm. Brian Rivers was Editor, Geoff Hibbins, Sports Editor, Jimmy Gray, Humour and Quiz sections. Alwyn Parsons and Jeff Long, Printers. After considering all the proposed names as its title, WOPPIN came out as the winner. Little did we realise when it was chosen, what a rumpus it would cause.

WOPPIN, First Edition, 1946. (Courtesy Jim Duthie)

In the Parish Magazine of September 1946, written by, not only the Vicar of St Peters, but also a member of the Boys Club management committee, The Rev Paul Rebbeck. He wrote 'Congratulations to Wolvercote Boys Club on the first number of it's new Magazine. Full of life, but who, or what is Woppin? Sounds like a relative of Chopin!' Brian Rivers nearly exploded when he read it, he was like a dog with a bone, he wouldn't let go. You have to bear in mind, that as Editor, the magazine was literally run by him. We all waited with baited breath for the next issue, would he retaliate?

We were not to be disappointed. Under the heading EDITORS NOTE appeared: Our Editorial staff has been greatly increased, so that we should be able to cater for all. While reading the Local Parish Magazine a short while ago, I came across a paragraph relating to the irrelevancy of our title WOPPIN, the writer of the paragraph had wondered if it had anything to do with the composer Chopin. Well first of all, I should like to remind the writer that the right pronunciation of Chopin, is Show-Pah, not Chopin. Actually, WOPPIN is a local abbreviation of Wolvercote, which has been in use for a number of years. Incidentally, I have received my calling up papers, so a new Editor will take over next month.

Rev Paul Rebbeck.

Brian Rivers

With Riv gone, Jeff Long and Alwyn Parsons moved from Printers to Joint Editors, their old positions were filled by Brian Taylor and Mick Rivers. So it was, that those of us who were between the ages of 18 to 20 years old were on borrowed time. National Service inevitably meant that everything was on the move, nothing remained the same for long.

A regular feature that appeared in WOPPIN, was FORCES CORNER. This did it's best to keep us up to date with the 'Old Boy's'.

A example of typical forces news, would be presented thus:

Wally Prescott on returning from leave, has been posted abroad.

Best wishes to Brian Rivers, Dingle Warwick and John Stockford, now in the Army. Little has been heard from Tubby Saxton, since he went abroad.

All the best to Arthur Dongworth who's off to India, and Eric Minns who's in Palestine. Pete Parker hopes to join the Fleet Air Arm.

Seen on leave during the last month.

Jim Crozier, John Cox, who has been moved to Bournemouth, means he has been separated from Roy Parsons, Dave Walker, Les Warwick, Wally Prescott, Stan Hopkins, Cyril Hopkins and Pickle Drewitt. Nice to see you lads. Good Luck.

And of course our best wishes to Frank Hill and Alwyn Parsons, due to go soon.

It became obvious that the comfort zone of friends who we had grown up with, were soon to be no more. As the saying goes, 'That was then, This is now'.

FORCES CORNER

Reg Buckle, R.A.F.

John Cox, Army.

Bill
Drewitt,
Army.

Fred
Drewett,
Army para-
trooper.

John
Duffin,
R.A.F.

Wally
Prescott,
Army.

John
Simms,
R.A.F.

John
Stone,
Army.

Brian
Stone,
R.A.F.

Michael
Stockford,
R.A.F.P.

Les Warwick and John Stockford, Army.   Dave Walker, Army.

This to me is quite a historic picture. Due to it being the last time we would all be together, mainly because of National Service. I like others were unable to attend as it was taken when I had to attend Night School. Starting at the Back row, from left to right: Peter Parker, Bill Hiett, Roland Howard, Geoff Long, Les Waine, Reg Buckle, John Cox, Geoff Hibbins, Tom Dicks. Middle row: Alwyn Parsons, John Allen, Peter Walker, Brian Rivers, Sid Talbot, Ken Cavey, Tony Portman, ?, Bert Green, Ray Butler, Roy Parsons, ?, John Saxton, Perce Hambridge. Front row: Dennis Harding, John Payne, Bobby Gray, John Walton, Mick Rivers, Aubrey Dorrill, Vic Gascoyne, Eddie Gray, Joe O'Neill, Dave Walker, Frank Spiers.

The last time that we were all together was at camp in Sandown, Isle of Wight. Skip Martin will always be remembered by the lads of my generation for the huge effort he put in to ensure that, although money was short, there was so much to be gained by not only personal effort, but always consider the other man.

Sandown Camp, Isle of Wight, 1946.

One happy tent of campers in 1946. Back row, left to right: Gary Walker, Arthur Simmonds, Fred Fitzgerald, Roy Parsons. Front row: ?, Dave Walker, Pete Walker. (Courtesy June Gray)

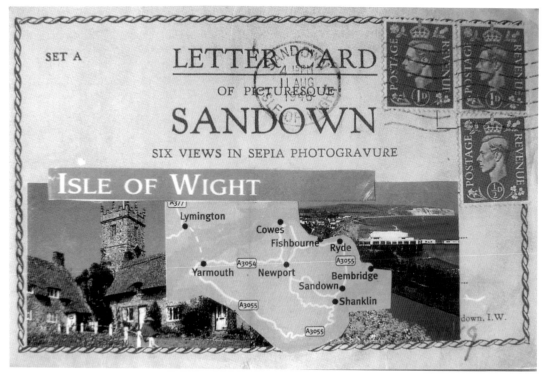

Letter card sent from camp, 11th August 1946.

Wolvercote Boys Club at a mixed camp, Brean Sands, 1950. The girls were from another club. Boys left to right: Bill Henton, Bob Mathews, Aubrey Dorrill, Keith Plato, Mick Soden, Tony Pratley, John Duffin, Bob Pratley, ?, Ron White. (Photo courtesy Kathleen Pratley, names John Duffin)

Albert Truman, ?, Mick Rivers, ?, John Cox, Kathy Crozier on a boys club outing, 1946. (Courtesy Kathy Rivers)

John Cox and John Stone in a relaxing mood, 1947.

John Kempson. M.B.E.

John Kempson received an M.B.E. from H.R.H. The Prince of Wales at Buckingham Palace in 2002 for services to the youth of Wolvercote and Oxfordshire. He retired in that year having served Wolvercote Boys and Young Peoples Club for 34 years. (Courtesy John Kempson)

I and so many other Wolvercote boys have so much to thank the Boys Club for, even today, over 65 years later, those of us, whenever we meet still talk fondly of our days at the club, thanks to John Kempson who in later years was the Skip Martin of his day, we meet at the reunions he organises. To them and all their contemporaries we can only say 'Thank you Wolvercote Boys Club for all you did for us, you did us proud, we are eternally grateful.'

Teenage Years

In the 1930s we were more than satisfied with what facilities there were around us, the need to venture further afield didn't seem necessary. With the Meadow; Railway; Canal and surrounding countryside on our doorstep, why bother to go anywhere else? We became more ambitious when we became the proud owner of our first 'big' bicycle, this would have been purchased from either Jack Cross in the Village or Eric Bonds shop in Summertown. With the main roads being comparatively free of motor traffic, and warnings from our parents to 'watch where we are going', we would pedal off to see what Summertown had to offer. This resulted in regular visits to A. S. Rising (known to all as Assy) and his Aladdin's cave of Hornby trains, Dinky toys and Meccano, he very rarely allowed us into his shop, we could view from outside providing we didn't touch the window. On the corner of Stratfield Road, South Parade, was a second-hand shop that sold furniture and bric-a-brac, his name was Egbert Taylor. We would rummage through his 'bargain boxes'. With nothing in them for a penny, we would leave. Another good old 'rummager' was on the left hand side of the entrance to Alexandra Park from George Street (now Middle Way) it was so cluttered you could barely move, I can only remember buying one thing from there, that being a cut glass stopper for a decanter. I liked the rainbow colours you could see when you held it up to the light, that, and the fact it only cost a penny.

It was vitally important that whatever 'spending spree' we had been on, to arrive at our next port of call with the necessary tuppence ha'penny. This was for a bag of broken bits from Oliver & Gurden's, a notice affixed to the wall at high level, clearly visible to all, proclaimed 'The Manufacturer of Quality Confectionery'. We didn't disagree with that, our 'prize' was a bag of bits, this consisted of cakes and tarts that were either broken or didn't come under their 'High Class' image, we weren't proud. You hit the jackpot if you finished up with a bag of squashed chocolate date tarts, the other end of the scale was nothing but maderia cake crumbs. It wasn't a question of just walking into the shop, you would have to queue for ages, time and again you would arrive at the shop door, only to be told "Sorry, sold out, come back next Saturday."

My Aunt Chris was employed by Oliver & Gurden's. The business was founded in 1919 by two former chefs from Keble College, William Oliver and Aubrey Gurden, their aim from the beginning was to produce quality cakes at a affordable price, in this they certainly succeeded. From modest premises in George Street, it eventually occupied the area from Alexandra Park as far along on the West side to almost opposite Grove Street, from using Grimbly Hughes and Twinings as the main source of sales, the quality of their cakes soon spread, so much so that in 1937 T. H. Kingerlee & Sons were employed to build a further extension to the already considerable premises, bringing the total number of employees to just over 100.

Oliver & Gurden's Staff, 1937. Chris Rooke (later Stockford), 2nd left in front row.

A. E. Gurden seated centre front row. Chris Rooke, left hand end front row with some of Oliver & Gurden's Staff, 1937.

Oliver & Gurden's fleet of vans, 1936.

Advert showing Christmas Cakes decorated by Chris Rooke, 1937.

Messrs Oliver & Gurden with Company letterhead 1937.

Oliver & Gurden's Shop, seen in centre of photo, 1937.

Post-war queue for 'Bag of bits', 1946.

Many of which were from Wolvercote. Arthur Taylor being one, he always boasted that he was born on the same day as Queen Elizabeth which made him special, he was employed as a van driver and made deliveries over a wide area. I, together with his son Tony were frequent passengers, the attraction being more for the cakes we had, rather than admiring the scenery.

Aunt Chris was the senior 'special cakes' decorator. Wedding, Birthday and Christmas cakes being her speciality. I didn't gain any freebies from that source! Where things paid off was Easter-time, as she was also the leading Easter-egg decorater, any that were not up to scratch were classed as 'seconds' which you could obtain for sixpence, her pride would not allow her to admit, that every egg she decorated was anything less than perfect, hence, no 'seconds'. Christmas Puddings was another delicious item they produced, they were so popular it became necessary to make them all year round to keep up with the demand.

From modest beginnings they grew into world-wide suppliers. Like so many other things, with the introduction of Supermarkets, demand for such quality products went into decline. To everyone's dismay they were taken over by Scribbons-Kemp in 1961. "What goes round, comes round" as the old saying goes, and in 1969 they themselves were taken over by Lyons. Like all big take-overs, things never seem to work out and the old Oliver & Gurden's factory closed down. Wolvercote people will always remember them, not only for their quality, but above all, their tuppence-ha'penny bag of bits.

Although only 30 years separated Oliver & Gurden's in it's prime from the beginning of the century, it must have seemed more like 300 years to the Wolvercote people who were in the early years of married lives at the turn of the century. The following is a typical weekly household expenditure for a H. O. King employee: Bacon 3d; Fish 3d; Beef 1/1d; Chops 4d; Meat-scraps 6d; Pig-pudding 1d; Liver 2½d, Dripping 3d; Potatoes 6d; Greens 2d; Celery 1d; Cheese 3d; Flour & Milk 3d; Cake 2½d; Bread 4d; Tea 6d; Cocoa 2d; 7 x 2 lb Loaves @ 2½d each = 1/5½d; Milk for week 7d; Butter 6d; Oil 4d; Coal 1/-; Wood 3½d; Minding baby 1/6d; Insurance 9d; Rent 2/6d; Total: 14/4d. His weekly wage was 12/- per week, his wife working as a char was earning 4/- per week, bringing their total income to 16/- a week, this left them with 1/8d, for clothes and other household expenses other than the bare necessities of life, this was with just one child. It beggars belief as to how they managed when more children came along. That was in 1909, what of 1939? How were things different?

Although the two Railway Holts were no more, we had a regular bus service with the Number 4 Bus, the stops were more regular then, the service would alternate in those days. Upper Wolvercote service would start at the roundabout, those living on the St Peters road estate had the choice of First Turn stop. An alternative was across the back of the school, over the level crossing, through the rabbit gate (where Bladon Close now is), and catch the bus at Davenant Road stop. This alternated with Lower Wolvercote which ran down Godstow Road via the Woodstock Road roundabout to the terminus by the green in front of the Red Lion. There was no side road service, so whichever part of the village you lived in you had a fair old trek to catch the bus into Oxford. The fare was 2½d, collected by a bus conductor, popularly known as a 'Clippy'. Having arrived in town, what were their favourite shops? I mentioned earlier how much Grimbly Hughes was a favourite, you could buy almost all your groceries from there, it was usual to go down Market Street to the Covered Market as your next port of call to complete your food shopping. All of the shopkeepers seemed to know all their customers by name, always with a smile and a 'Thank you for calling', as you left the shop. Depending who I went shopping with made a big difference to what shop we visited, as a boy living in a pub meant that it was not possible for both mother and father to go together. As somebody had to stay at home to look after the pub it was normal for mother to do her shopping on a Tuesday, when she would catch the No. 4 bus, which naturally limited to what she could carry. During term time at school it meant she was on her own, at holiday time I invariably accompanied her, this would be when shopping for other than food took place.

Popular shops were Elliston & Cavell in Magdalen Street, this was usually followed by a visit to Webbers in High Street, by which time I'd had enough, as there was very little in either shop that I was interested in. "What are we coming here for," I would wail, to which mother would reply. "Ladies things." To keep me quiet she would promise to take me into the Drugstore in Cornmarket Street on the way home and let me choose a new Dinky Toy, a promise that always worked as it was a truly wonderful shop, stocked with every MECCANO product you could dream of, depending what craze I was 'into' at the time decided on my 'reward'. A ship would start at a penny, a aeroplane or a car at 4d. I never pushed my luck and always started at the bottom, that way things could get better. The one shop I was always more than pleased to visit was Capes down St Ebbe's, it wasn't so much what they sold, the attraction was the overhead cash system there. You paid at the counter where the assistant would put your money into a container which was attached to a overhead wire, pull a chain that hung down, causing the container to shoot off like a rocket to a central cash desk where a cashier would issue a receipt, put the change in the container and send it back by the same method, all of which took no more than a minute.

Webbers, High Street store, 1947.

Elliston & Cavell Ltd, to the left hand side is C. Taphouse & Son where Rikki Durgess would serve us when we could scrape up 1/6d to purchase our favourite 78 r.p.m. record.

In boxed condition, 1939. This lot would fetch £1,000 today.

Capes and G. R. Cooper, Ironmongers (known as the dustpan) in St Ebbe's Street, as seen from Queen Street, 1914.

Interior of Capes, unfortunately the overhead cash system is not visible, 1927.

Licenced Victualler Annual Dinner, Seacourt Arms, Botley, 1937. Back row, left to right: Margaret Willey, Jack Stockford, ?, ?, ?, ?, Jack Allaway, Mrs Allaway, ?. Front row: ?, ?, Gert Willey, ?, ?, Frank Ayres, Arthur Willey.

Oxford Milk Bar, George Street, 1949.

Electra Cinema,
Queen Street, 1938.
Site now occupied by
Marks & Spencer.

Laurel & Hardy, our film favourite's, 1937.

Wireless and film favourite's, Moore Marriot, ' Stinker ' Murdoch, Arthur Askey, Graham Moffatt, 1942.

Shopping with father was a lot different as his was what he referred to as 'business shopping'. He would always use his car to collect his telephoned orders, the route to Oxford would invariably be via Walton Street where we would stop off at Tom Taylors for a haircut. A little further on he would call into the Clarendon Arms with. "I won't be a minute. I'll just see how Sid Judge is getting on". Half an hour later he would emerge to say that if we didn't stop hanging about we would never get to see Aubrey Plested. He owned the Candy Stores down St Ebbe's and supplied the items that we sold in the Jug & Bottle, such as crisps, biscuits, and nuts & raisins, all to be sold at 2d a packet. Having seen us pull up. Aubrey would approach us with a jar of sweets under his arm, unscrewing the top he then offered them to me saying "Take a hand full Michael". I didn't have to be told twice. With the exception of Aubrey, Father's 'shopping' would mainly incorporate his Licence Victualler (licenced landlord of a Public House) mates. Next stop would be at Morrells Brewery to pay his bill to Colonel Morrell as Father always called him.

If I needed new boots (never shoes) they would be from Freeman, Hardy & Willis, on the corner of New in Hall and Queen Streets. Clothes would be from Zacharias & Co. in Cornmarket St. "Let's call in and see Billy King," he would say. Two visits stand out in my mind. One, was to be measured for a new long trousered suit (my first) to be ready for my Confirmation. The second, to buy a new swagger Mackintosh coat, it lasted for years and never wore out, I just outgrew it. When we came out of the shop, he would 'nip in for a quick one' with Perce Chapman who kept the Northgate Tavern opposite.

Depending on who he wanted to visit next, would determine our route home. I visited more Pubs in my childhood than I have in my entire adult life. We either called in the Shotover Arms at Headington, popular with me, as there was a model Hornby train layout that ran round the Saloon Bar. If our route took us down the Abingdon Rd, the stop would be at the Farriers Arms, run by Frank Ayres. A great friend of fathers was Arthur Willey at The Seacourt Arms on the Botley Rd, this invariably won. With the only way home from there being Wytham, the final stop would be Harry Hastings, landlord of the White Hart in Wolvercote. Obviously a lot of business had to be discussed!

As kids we seldom went down Oxford unaccompanied, on the odd occasion when we did it was usually for a special occasion such as a military parade or similar.

When we became teenagers and could earn the odd Half Crown it more often than not burnt a hole in our pocket which resulted in a visit to the Milk Bar followed by the cinema, or 'pictures' as we called it.

The Oxford (later called The Super) together with The Ritz showed the latest releases. British films were our favourites, especially the war films. American films were mainly musicals with Betty Grable, Rita Hayworth, June Haver and the like, invariably they would walk down a large staircase singing some soppy song.

No such problem with the Electra in Queen Street as the films shown there were more often than not years old and of a 'B' Certificate, suitable for a captive audience of kids like us. Laurel & Hardy, Will Hay, Moore Marriott, Graham Moffatt, Arthur Askey, George Formby and Abbot & Costello were huge favourites and always good for a laugh.

George Formby, 1942. Over a
four year period, he was a
box-office favourite.

Abbot & Costello, 1942.
We would queue for hours
to see their films.

Big Bill Campbell, Rocky Mountain
Rhythm 'Mighty Fine', 'Mighty Fine',
1942.

New Theatre Programme,
price 3d, 1942.

The ever present constable on Carfax point duty, he appears to have more pedestrians to control than traffic, 1935.

The Oxford, renamed the Super and now the Odeon cinema in Magdalen Street, 1937.

The Oxford Ice Rink, Botley Road, 1935. Being as it didn't pay it was turned into The Majestic Cinema.

The old Ice Rink on the Botley Road - transformed into the Majestic Cinema showed films we had seen so many times you knew what was coming. The acoustics were truly awful. With a auditorium packed with yelling kids you couldn't hear a word. At the other end of the scale you had the New Theatre. When Big Bill Campbell and his Rocky Mountain Rhythm was on it was always followed by 'Mighty Fine -Mighty Fine' which was his catch phrase. One very special treat we all enjoyed was a visit with the choir to see Snow White & the Seven Dwarfs. The first full length cartoon film ever made. As it was considered to be so important and suitable for children it was shown at the New Theatre. I was not alone in having nightmares over the Wicked Queen! Overall the pictures were good value in those days. You had two type of films known as a 'A' certificate (you had to be over the age of 18) or a ` B' if you were under that age. A programme would consist of two films, a cartoon, a trailer for the next weeks films and the Movitone News. If you were up to it you could see the whole lot twice as the programme was continuous.

Having left school we set about making our mark in the world. Those of us serving apprenticeships attended night school at least four nights a week. A dance at the Village Hall for 1/6d was a popular meeting place, as we became more confident we tried our skills at the Carfax Assembly Rooms or the Town Hall on a Saturday night.

A legacy from the American GIs was jitterbugging or jiving as it became known. Although popular it was banned in most places. The majority of us were not very proficient on the dance floor and settled for the 'Hokey Cokey' or 'Do you know the Muffin Man'. No-one ever considered meeting in a pub, if we arranged to meet for a drink it was usually at the Milk Bar in George Street, with a milk shake costing 10d, it was always a special treat. Other than the Boys Club it was a venue where we would meet up along with our girl-friends, all of which were mainly Wolvercote or Summertown girls.

All this changed with a vengeance when we reached the age of 18 and we were off to serve King and Country for 2 years. We didn't realise it at the time, but that was for so many of us the last time (in many cases), that we would see one another, for possibly decades. As a result of my previous book, 'Growing up in Wolvercote, 1931-1951'. It has brought so many memories back to Wolvercote people (both Upper and Lower), who have taken the trouble to contact me to share not only their memories, but their memorabilia, that in many cases has made it into quite a emotional journey. To hear from those who as a boy I was very close to, and not having seen them for over half a century has made the journey so rewarding. It's been a two way experience, as memories locked away for decades have been brought into the open.

My sincere thanks to all who have been so generous in contacting me from the four corners of the globe. Wolvercote truly is a place that holds so many memories for us. As children Wolvercote seemingly offered all we required to keep us amused. I don't think we were very demanding, no more than our parents were, they like us were content with a lot less than we enjoy today, like us they had each other.

In a recent letter from my brother he agreed with me when he concluded 'all these wonderful happy memories of our childhood which children today would not begin to understand.' When I look back on growing up in Wolvercote it was a wonderfully happy time. We had everything we wanted within our reach, the Thames, the canal, the railway, the meadows and truly great people. What more could a growing child want.